questioning identity

AN INTRODUCTION TO THE SOCIAL SCIENCES: UNDERSTANDING SOCIAL CHANGE

This book is part of a series produced in association with The Open University. The complete list of books in the series is as follows:

The books form part of the Open University course DD100 *An Introduction to the Social Sciences: Understanding Social Change*. Details of this and other Open University courses can be obtained from the Course Reservations Centre, PO Box 724, The Open University, Milton Keynes MK7 6ZS, United Kingdom: tel. +44 (0)1908 653231, e-mail ces-gen@open.ac.uk

Alternatively, you may visit the Open University website at http://www.open.ac.uk where you can learn more about the wide range of courses and packs offered at all levels by The Open University.

For availability of other course components, contact Open University Worldwide Ltd, The Berrill Building, Walton Hall, Milton Keynes MK7 6AA, United Kingdom: tel. +44 (0)1908 858785; fax +44 (0)1908 858787; e-mail ouwenq@open.ac.uk; website http://www.ouw.co.uk

questioning identity: gender, class, nation

edited by kath woodward

London and New York

in association with

The Open University

First published 2000 by Routledge; written and produced by The Open University
11 New Fetter Lane, London EC4P 4EE

Simultaneously published in the USA and Canada by Routledge
29 West 35th Street, New York, NY 10001

Routledge is an imprint of the Taylor & Francis Group

Edited, designed and typeset by The Open University.

Printed by The Bath Press, Bath.

British Library Cataloguing in Publication Data
A catalogue record for this book is available from The British Library

Library of Congress Cataloging in Publication Data
A catalogue record for this book has been requested

ISBN 0-415-22287-7 (hbk)

ISBN 0-415-22288-5 (pbk)

1.1

Contents

The Open University course team

John Allen, *Senior Lecturer in Geography*

Penny Bennett, *Editor*

Pam Berry, *Compositor*

Simon Bromley, *Senior Lecturer in Government*

David Calderwood, *Project Controller*

Elizabeth Chaplin, *Tutor Panel*

Giles Clark, *Co-publishing Advisor*

Stephen Clift, *Editor*

Allan Cochrane, *Professor of Public Policy*

Lene Connolly, *Print Buying Controller*

Graham Dawson, *Lecturer in Economics*

Lesley Duguid, *Senior Course Co-ordination Secretary*

Ross Fergusson, *Staff Tutor in Social Policy*

Fran Ford, *Senior Course Co-ordination Secretary*

David Goldblatt, *Co-Course Team Chair, Lecturer in Government*

Jenny Gove, *Lecturer in Psychology*

Judith Greene, *Professor of Psychology*

Montserrat Guibernau, *Lecturer in Government*

Peter Hamilton, *Lecturer in Sociology*

Celia Hart, *Picture Researcher*

David Held, *Professor of Politics and Sociology*

Susan Himmelweit, *Senior Lecturer in Economics*

Steve Hinchliffe, *Lecturer in Geography*

Gordon Hughes, *Lecturer in Social Policy*

Christina Janoszka, *Course Manager*

Pat Jess, *Staff Tutor in Geography*

Bob Kelly, *Staff Tutor in Government*

Margaret Kiloh, *Staff Tutor in Applied Social Sciences*

Sylvia Lay-Flurrie, *Secretary*

Siân Lewis, *Graphic Designer*

Tony McGrew, *Professor of International Relations, University of Southampton*

Hugh Mackay, *Staff Tutor in Sociology*

Maureen Mackintosh, *Professor of Economics*

Eugene McLaughlin, *Senior Lecturer in Applied Social Science*

Andrew Metcalf, *Senior Producer, BBC*

Gerry Mooney, *Staff Tutor in Applied Social Sciences*

Ray Munns, *Graphic Artist*

Kathy Pain, *Staff Tutor in Geography*

Clive Pearson, *Tutor Panel*

Lynne Poole, *Tutor Panel*

Norma Sherratt, *Staff Tutor in Sociology*

Roberto Simonetti, *Lecturer in Economics*

Dick Skellington, *Project Officer*

Brenda Smith, *Staff Tutor in Psychology*

Mark Smith, *Lecturer in Social Sciences*

Grahame Thompson, *Professor of Political Economy*

Ken Thompson, *Professor of Sociology*

Stuart Watt, *Lecturer in Psychology/KMI*

Andy Whitehead, *Graphic Artist*

Kath Woodward, *Co-Course Team Chair, Staff Tutor in Sociology*

Chris Wooldridge, *Editor*

External Assessor

Nigel Thrift, *Professor of Geography, University of Bristol*

Series preface

Questioning Identity: Gender, Class, Nation is the first in a series of five books, entitled *An Introduction to the Social Sciences: Understanding Social Change*. If the social sciences are to retain and extend their relevance in the twenty-first century there can be little doubt that they will have to help us understand social change. In the 1990s an introductory course to the social sciences would have looked completely different.

From a global perspective it appears that the pace of change is quickening, social and political ideas and institutions are under threat. The international landscape has changed; an intensification of technological change across computing, telecommunications, genetics and biotechnology present new political, cultural and moral dilemmas and opportunities. Real intimations of a global environmental crisis in the making have emerged. We are, it appears, living in an uncertain world. We are in new territory.

The same is also true of more local concerns. At the beginning of the twenty-first century both societies and the social sciences are in a state of flux. *Understanding Social Change* has been written at a moment that reflects, albeit in a partial way, subterranean shifts in the social and cultural character of the UK. Established social divisions and social identities of class, gender, ethnicity and nation are fragmenting and re-forming. Core institutions such as the family, work and welfare have become more diverse and complex. It is also a moment when significant processes of change have been set in train – such as constitutional reform and European economic and monetary union – whose longer-term trajectory remains uncertain. The flux in the social sciences has been tumultuous. Social change, uncertainty and diversity have rendered many of the most well-established frameworks in the social sciences of limited use and value. Social change on this scale demands fresh perspectives and new systems of explanation.

In this context *Understanding Social Change* is part of a bold and innovative educational project, for it attempts to capture and explore these processes of momentous social change and in doing so reasserts the utility and necessity of the social sciences. Each of the five books which make up the series attempts precisely this, and they all do so from a fundamentally interdisciplinary perspective. Social change is no respecter of the boundaries of disciplines and the tidy boxes that social scientists have often tried to squeeze it into. Above all, *Understanding Social Change* seeks to maintain and extend the Open University's democratic educational mission: to reach and enthuse an enormously diverse student population; to insist that critical, informed, reflexive engagement with the direction of social change is not a matter for elites and professional social scientists alone.

As you may have guessed, this series of books forms a core component of the Open University, Faculty of Social Sciences, level 1 course, DD100 *An Introduction to the Social Sciences: Understanding Social Change*. Each book in the series can be read independently of the other books and independently from the rest of the materials that make up the Open University course. However, if you wish to use the series as a whole, there are a number of references to chapters in other books in the series, and these are easily identifiable because they are printed in bold type.

Making the course and these books has been a long and complex process, and thanks are due to an enormous number of people.

First and foremost, the entire project has been managed and kept on the rails, when it was in mortal danger of flying off them, by our excellent Course Manager, Christina Janoszka. In the DD100 office, Fran Ford, Lesley Duguid and Sylvia Lay-Flurrie have been the calm eye at the centre of a turbulent storm, our thanks to all of them.

Stephen Clift, Chris Wooldridge and Penny Bennett have been meticulous, hawk-eyed editors. Siân Lewis has provided superb design work, and Ray Munns and Andy Whitehead have provided skilled cartographic and artistic work. David Calderwood in project control has arranged and guided the schedule with calm efficiency and Celia Hart has provided great support with illustrations and photographs. Nigel Thrift, our external assessor, and Clive Pearson, Elizabeth Chaplin and Lynne Poole, our tutor panel, have provided consistent and focused criticism, support and advice. Peggotty Graham has been an invaluable friend of *Understanding Social Change* and David Held has provided balance, perspective and insight as only he can.

It only remains for us to say that we hope you find *Understanding Social Change* an engaging and illuminating introduction to the social sciences, and in turn you find the social sciences essential for understanding life in the twenty-first century.

David Goldblatt
Kath Woodward
Co-Chairs, The Open University Course Team

Introduction

Kath Woodward

> We live in a world where identity matters. It matters both as a concept, theoretically, and as a contested fact of contemporary political life.
>
> (Gilroy, 1997, p.301)

Why is identity of interest to social scientists? Why does it matter now? The discussion of identity in this book is organized around three central questions, although each of these questions provokes further lines of enquiry. The first question is: *how are identities formed?* Identities are formed through interaction between people. When people take up different identities there are different processes taking place as people position themselves, and are positioned, in the social world. These processes include a focus on the personal dimensions of the identity equation as well as an interrogation of how these connect to the society in which we live. Casting a spotlight on the social aspects of identity leads us to explore the structures through which our lives are organized. Our identities are shaped by social structures but we also participate in forming our own identities. Which are the more important of these structures? We suggest that gender, class and culture (using the example of nation) are particularly important. These are introduced in Chapter 1 and become respectively the focus of Chapters 2, 3 and 4. We explore some of the processes involved when people interact with each other and the world around them.

Discussion of the role of social factors in identity formation raises the second framing question: *to what extent can we shape our own identities?* The changes which are identified are largely structural: in the economy, in new technologies, through migration and ethnic diversity, in the organization of domestic and family life, and in gender roles. How far do these structures constrain people and shape their identities and to what extent are people able to reconstruct themselves and their own identities? How can people influence social structures and use them to recreate collective identities? Identity necessarily involves an interrelationship between the personal and the social which can also be expressed as a tension between structure and agency. This tension is a key concern of the book.

The third framing question is: *are there particular uncertainties about identity at this moment in the UK?* There have been significant changes in forms of domestic living, family life and employment in the post-war period. Recent years have seen a proliferation of new technologies and communication systems which might appear to open up the possibility of transforming our daily lives. Such changes take place at the global level but have an impact on the UK. The structure of the UK is changing politically with devolution, separate assemblies and more explicit recognition of the political identities of

Wales, Scotland and Northern Ireland. The UK is a multicultural society with a diverse ethnic population which challenges the notion that being British means being white. Identities are changing and fluid and this very fluidity creates uncertainty and diversity, but what forms does the expression of uncertainty take? What possibilities are there for reconstruction through the formation of new identities? How do we seek to stabilize identities at a time of change and disruption?

Each of the three framing questions is about finding out and about producing knowledge, upon which it is possible to make claims about identity. This involves an introduction to some of the methods adopted by social scientists, as well as some discussion of the production of knowledge through culture – for example, through symbols such as language and visual images. Throughout the book we extend a social science critique which starts with questions which lead to claims, building up arguments by citing evidence which is then evaluated. Each chapter revisits the claims made in previous chapters and reconsiders the need for more evidence and different questions. The book as a whole thus develops cumulatively, with each chapter exploring different claims and seeking more evidence and developing explanations about how identities are formed.

In Chapter 1, 'Questions of Identity', Kath Woodward sets the scene by introducing the three central questions of the book. This chapter focuses on definitions of identity and on what social science can tell us about the ways in which identities are formed and how individuals make sense of themselves in the social world in which they live. The chapter highlights some of the key dimensions of identity: the social structures which might shape our sense of who we are – gender, class and nation. They are often the site of contradictory and competing identities, but each offers the possibility of some grounding for our understanding of ourselves and opportunities for diversity through forging new identities in changing times. Different social science approaches give more or less emphasis to the agency which can be exercised in taking up identities, but all involve some interrelationship between the personal and the social. This chapter introduces some of the ways in which knowledge about identities is produced, through first-person evidence, visual images and representations, as well as through social science critiques which draw upon such evidence.

In Chapter 2, 'Identity and Gender', Jennifer Gove and Stuart Watt focus on gender as a key source of identity. Gender might be seen to offer some grounding for identity. Does it? Where might we look to find out if being female or male might offer some basis for understanding the identities which people have? The first part of the chapter looks at what gender categories mean and how gender identities are formed in childhood. What sort of criteria do we use to classify people as women or as men and to distinguish between feminine and masculine behaviour? The chapter's focus on gendered performance in education offers a useful illustration both of change in a particular historical period (post-war to the present) and of apparent certainties, specifically boys' overachievement, being subverted and challenged by girls' recent success, for example, in public exams. This recent phenomenon, more complex than it at first appears, suggests both uncertainty and new opportunities and the possibility of restructuring gender stereotypes and forging new gender identities. Jennifer Gove and Stuart Watt consider the tensions between individual agency and social structures, especially the constraints of gender stereotypes and categories, in the shaping of gender identities. The chapter explores claims about gender categorization and looks at different sources of evidence, including empirical data, and at different theoretical explanations of gender difference.

In Chapter 3, 'Identity, Inequality and Social Class', Maureen Mackintosh and Gerry Mooney shift the focus on to the economic bases of identity and extend earlier discussion of difference to concentrate on inequality. At a time of change in patterns of employment in the UK, work-based identities are changing and may offer more uncertainty, as does the challenge to social class as a major determinant of who we are. However, economic factors, in particular poverty, must surely offer a bottom line in determining who we are. Or is the picture here more complex? The chapter explores some different social science explanations of class, drawing on the work of Karl Marx and Max Weber, and goes on to consider ways in which individuals and groups might actively engage in shaping their own identities. This introduces more recent debates about the relationship between production and consumption and the importance of lifestyle, where people, through the practice of consumption, can be seen as consuming identities.

In Chapter 4, 'Identity and Nation', Montserrat Guibernau and David Goldblatt move the spotlight again to address another dimension of identity which has particular historical resonance, reflected in the changes taking place in the UK. Why is nation important in the construction of collective identities and what processes are involved in the creation of these identities? National identities are formed through historical processes and the stories we tell ourselves about the nation. Where do these stories come from? What are the origins of our ideas about Britishness, for example? These stories are told through symbols and re-enacted through rituals. This chapter extends Chapter 1's discussion of the importance of representations in the formation of identity. Is there more uncertainty about being British, or English, or Scottish, or Welsh, or Irish at this time? Are there more opportunities for the creation of new ethnic identities through multiculturalism and ethnic diversity or is there greater fragmentation and uncertainty?

The book is question led, as can be seen from the title! This is in keeping with the development of the critical approach to social science. Our approach is genuinely interdisciplinary. Those of us writing in this book come from the disciplines of sociology, politics, psychology, economics and social policy and draw on the analyses of our own disciplines as well as recent interdisciplinary critiques of identity.

Reference

Gilroy, P. (1997) 'Diaspora and the detours of identity' in Woodward, K. (ed.) *Identity and Difference*, London, Sage/The Open University.

Questions of identity

Kath Woodward

chapter 1

Contents

1 QUESTIONS OF IDENTITY

This chapter is about questions of identity. Identity itself seems to be about a question, 'who am I?' We are going to focus on three key questions:

- How are identities formed?

- How much control do we have in shaping our own identities?

- Are there particular uncertainties about identity in the contemporary UK?

First, we need to think a bit more about what we mean by identity.

1.1 What is identity?

If identity provides us with the means of answering the question 'who am I?' it might appear to be about personality; the sort of person I am. That is only part of the story. Identity is different from personality in important respects. We may share personality traits with other people, but sharing an identity suggests some *active* engagement on our part. We choose to *identify* with a particular identity or group. Sometimes we have more choice than others. This chapter will address the relative importance of *structures*, the forces beyond our control which shape our identities, and *agency*, the degree of control which we ourselves can exert over who we are. Identity requires some awareness on our part. Personality describes qualities individuals may have, such as being outgoing or shy, internal characteristics, but identity requires some element of choice. For example, I may go to football matches on Saturdays because I enjoy shouting loudly with a crowd of lively extroverts, but I go to watch Sheffield Wednesday because I want to *identify* with that particular team, to wear that scarf and make a statement about who I am, and, of course, because I want to state that I support *one* Sheffield team and *not* the other (Sheffield United). We may be characterized by having personality traits, but we have to identify with – that is, actively take up – an identity.

This example also illustrates the importance of marking oneself as having the *same* identity as one group of people and a *different* one from others. Think about a situation where you meet someone for the first time and, in trying to find out who they are, ask questions about where they come from and what they do. In such situations we are trying to find out what makes up this person and also what makes them the *same* as us – that is, what we have in common – and what makes them *different*. If you see somebody wearing the badge of an organization to which you also belong, it marks that person out as being the same as you, as sharing an identity. Or consider a situation where, travelling abroad, hearing the voices of those who speak your own language, you feel both a sense of recognition and of belonging. In a strange place, finding people who share our language provides us with something and someone with whom we can identify. Or imagine that you are on a train, and a stranger in the compartment is reading the local newspaper from the town where you were born. You might strike up a conversation which includes references to what you have in common. This presents a moment of recognition and of having something in common with another person who shares an identity with you. Identity is marked by similarity, that is of the people like us, and by difference, of those who are not. There are other examples which are less reassuring, where the appropriate identity is *not* established, and where, for example, one may be denied access to credit or hire purchase, pension or sickness benefits, or entry to a club or restaurant, or, even more significantly, to a country.

How do we know which people are the same as us? What information do we use to categorize others and ourselves? In the examples above, what is often important is a *symbol*, like a badge, a team scarf, a newspaper, the language we speak, or perhaps the clothes we wear. Sometimes it is obvious. A badge can be a clear public statement that we identify with a particular group. Sometimes it is more subtle, but symbols and representations are important in marking the ways in which we share identities with some people and distinguish ourselves as different from others.

In this sense, although as individuals we have to take up identities actively, those identities are necessarily the product of the society in which we live and our relationship with others. Identity provides a link between individuals and the world in which they live. Identity combines how I see myself and how others see me. Identity involves the internal and the subjective, and the external. It is a socially recognized position, recognized by others, not just by me.

However, how I see myself and how others see me do not always fit. For example, individuals may view themselves as high achievers, worthy of promotion, yet be viewed by their employer as less than successful. The young people noisily returning home from a club in the early hours of the morning may be seen by others as troublemakers. Think about some of the ways in which how you see yourself may be at variance with others' perception of you. This could be at a more personal level, in the context of family and friendship relationships, or at a more public or even global level, where particular characteristics are attributed to specific national or ethnic groups. A sense of conflicting identities may result from the tensions between having to be a student, a parent, and an employee at the same time: these are examples of the *multiple identities* which people have.

The link between myself and others is not only indicated by the connection between how I see myself and how other people see me, but also by the connection between what I want to be and the influences, pressures and opportunities which are available. Material, social and physical constraints prevent us from successfully presenting ourselves in some identity positions – constraints which include the perceptions of others. Criminal identities are often produced through the exaggeration of stereotyping, where newspaper reports reproduce the notion of a criminal identity as young, male and black (Mooney *et al.*, 2000). Criminality can be produced by others who construct this category of person. This process of stereotyping certain groups as criminal also illustrates some of the imbalances and inequalities in the relationship between the individual and the world outside.

The subject, 'I' or 'we' in the identity equation, involves some element of choice, however limited. The concept of identity encompasses some notion of human agency; an idea that we can have some control in constructing our own identities. There are, of course, constraints which may lie in the external world, where material and social factors may limit the degree of agency which individuals may have. Lack of material resources severely limits the opportunities we have, as we will consider in the case of poverty and economic constraints in Chapter 3. It is impossible to have an identity as a successful career woman if one is without a job and if there are no employment opportunities. Other limitations to our autonomy may reside within us, for example in the bodies which we inhabit, as illustrated by the ageing process, by physical impairments, illness and the actual size and shape of our bodies.

SUMMARY

Identity involves:

- a link between the personal and the social;
- some active engagement by those who take up identities;
- being the same as some people and different from others, as indicated by symbols and representations;
- a tension between how much control I have in constructing my identities and how much control or constraint is exercised over me.

2 WHO AM I?

• •

Let us start with an example of an individual and his identity which illustrates the link between the personal and the social. The social scientist Madan Sarup uses the example of his passport, which gives information about his identity in an official sense. Our passports name, describe and place us. A passport describes an individual; it names *one* person. It also states to which *group*, in particular which nation, that person belongs:

> I have three passports, all British ... In the first one, I am a young man with a lot of hair and a confident smile. My height is 5ft 8in and I am a school teacher. In my second passport photograph, most of the hair has gone. I have a white beard and a serious expression. My height is now 1.73 metres and I am a college lecturer. In the

third passport, the smaller red one, I am bald. Again I have a serious expression, but now my face is heavily lined. A friend asks: which is the *real* you? Of course, people see me in many different ways ... I want to have a closer look at my red passport ... At the top are the words 'European community' ... The passport refers to my nationality – British Citizen.

(Sarup, 1996, p.xiv)

FIGURE 1.1   Examples of UK passports

Three passports offer details about identities, which are different, yet each belongs to the same person. Physical appearance is important, but it changes over time. Sarup's friend asks, 'which is the real you?' This suggests that there is not only continuity in the name of the person who possesses the passports, but that there might be a fixed, true, 'real' identity which could be uncovered. The personal identity of the named person includes their experience and life story. Continuity is important to our understanding of who we are, but changes suggest that identities are not fixed and constant; they change too.

We have some information here about what Sarup looks like. At one level physical appearance is how we 'read' people when we meet them. The body is also an important component of personal identity. Sarup cites physical appearance as the principal example of what is revealed here, but there are many other aspects of the body which have an impact on identity. Size, shape, disability, sex, all influence our experience of who we are and who we can be.

A passport picks out other key aspects of identity, which include occupation, nationality and age, all of which position us and give us a place in the society in which we live. However, it does not say anything about *how* we occupy these positions or about what they mean to us. We do not know how Sarup himself feels. Passport details cannot reveal a person's feelings. We need more information:

I think of [British Citizenship] as a formal category, because it does not express how I feel about it. I am not proud to be 'British'; it reminds me of the scars of imperialism, the days of the Raj. I feel more sympathetic to being a citizen of the

European Community, but here too I feel ambivalent. I would rather be a citizen of a federal European Community, but friends remind me that the concept of the 'Fortress Europe' is a Euro-centric strategy to maintain the power and privilege of the 'First World'.

(Sarup, 1996, p.xv)

Here Sarup suggests that he identifies more actively with being a European than a British citizen. To identify with a nation or group like this is to take up a *collective identity*. However, only one UK identity is offered by the passport. I notice that my own passport gives my place of birth, in Wales, but currently calls me a British and not a Welsh citizen. That Britain is a multi-ethnic, multicultural society is not acknowledged here either. Sarup refers to the colonial past which positions him in a particular relationship with 'Britishness'. This history is not recognized in the passport. The British Empire, however, used to have a place, with the old blue passport which referred to 'The United Kingdom of Great Britain and her Colonies', but the more recent EC and the new EU passports have no place for multi-ethnicity as yet. Those who hold the UK passport are grouped together as if we share one British identity. What we have in common is that we do not have another national identity (unless we have dual citizenship). We are not French or Chinese nationals. Identity is thus also marked by difference; that is, by indicating what we are not. We shall return to the importance of nation in the creation of identities in Chapter 4.

The very fact of having a passport at all confers identity. Particular passports provide rights of citizenship which are denied those who do not possess a passport at all. The passport illustrates some of the ways in which identities are institutionally constructed, and in this case the UK state, through legislation, plays a very powerful part in defining the identities of its citizens, especially in making some identities possible and others impossible. In the UK, birth has to be registered in order for the child to exist officially at all. Birth certificates, like death certificates, require that the person be classified as female or male. There is no alternative or scope for negotiation. At present, whatever an individual does in life to change their gender identity, the death certificate has to accord with the birth certificate, which cannot be changed retrospectively. Other examples of the official production and classification of an identity include ID cards, credit cards, membership cards, driving licences or any other sort of licence.

ACTIVITY 1.1

Think about your own passport or any other identity card or official document. What does it say about you? Does it suggest groups with whom you share an identity and those from whom you are different? Does this suggest several different identities? What is omitted? What is the importance of such institutional identities?

COMMENT

The kind of information revealed in an official document like a passport has many omissions about what identities and allegiances may be important in our daily lives. Fortunately, the state does not expose our political allegiances, community involvement, sexuality or status as a parent, although these also combine to produce our identities. The apparently single identity of citizenship leaves out all the contradictions about who we are and the multiplicity of identities each of us has.

Institutions like the state do have the power to restrict individual or collective freedom to adopt some identities. We probably do not think about these restrictions nor about national identity or citizenship very often, except when we are denied the rights associated with citizenship.

SUMMARY

- The passport example illustrates the tension between how I see myself and how I am seen by others, between the personal and the social.
- Institutions such as the state play an important role in constructing identities.
- Difference is very clearly marked in relation to national identity.
- Such official categories contain omissions and cannot fully accommodate the personal investment we have in our identities, nor the multiple identities we have.

In the next section we explore some of the ways in which social science can clarify some of the definitions of identity which have been offered and begin to address some of the questions which have been asked.

3   WHO ARE YOU? WHAT CAN SOCIAL SCIENCE TELL US?

In Sections 1 and 2, I argued that identity possessed the following characteristics:

- It links how I see myself and how others see me.
- It links the individual and the social.
- It is marked by similarity and difference.
- It involves some active engagement on our part and a tension between human agency and social structures.

- There are single and multiple identities.
- Identities can be seen as fixed or fluid and changing.

In this section we return to the definition of identity and ask how social scientists have attempted to address these two questions:

How are identities formed?

How much control do we have in the construction of our identities?

3.1   Imagining ourselves

The work of the social philosopher George Herbert Mead, published in the 1930s, has been extensively used in thinking about identity because he offered useful insights into the link between how we see ourselves and the ability of human beings to *imagine* how others might see us (Mead, 1934). Think about it this way. Imagine that you have an interview for a job. You think about the interview before the 'big day' and consider what to wear. You want to look smart but perhaps that new suit would be too hot and you would end up feeling, and looking, very uncomfortable, especially if the heating was turned up high. Maybe you should try not to look too formal? What is going on here? In order to make the decision about what to wear you have to imagine yourself, to look at yourself from the outside. Mead argued that it is the capacity to imagine how others would see us and our capacity to carry images in our heads which is an important distinguishing feature of human beings. We do this, he argued, through **symbolizing**. This is best illustrated in our use of language, where words operate as symbols. Pictures, images and gestures are also symbolic in that they too *represent* something else. A symbol stands for something else. For example, the word 'table' stands for the object which we call a table. Having the word allows us to talk and think about the object, namely the table, even when there is no table within view. The suit worn at the interview in the scenario above signifies or stands for the serious candidate. We symbolize the sort of person we want others to think we are through the clothes we wear and the ways in which we behave. In the interview example we have an image of ourselves at the interview, either in the disastrous overheated scenario or preferably in another more confident, successful scene where we might *visualize* ourselves appropriately dressed and getting the job.

Symbolizing
Making one object, word or image stand for or signify another. For example, a red light at traffic lights symbolizes 'stop', and green means 'you can go'.

Symbols and representations are important in the production of identities. This is how we signal our identities to others and how we know which people we identify with and those who are distinguished as being different. How we speak, the clothes we wear, badges, scarves, uniforms or flags all offer symbols of identity. Judith Williamson, whose work focuses on representational systems, writing within the discipline of cultural studies, describes the process of choosing an identity in the following way:

When I rummage through my wardrobe in the morning I am not merely faced with the choice of what to wear. I am faced with the choice of images: the difference between a smart suit and a pair of overalls, a leather skirt and a cotton skirt, is not one of fabric and style, but one of identity. You know perfectly well that you will be seen differently for the whole day, depending on what you put on; you will appear as a particular kind of woman with one particular identity which excludes others. The black leather skirt rather rules out girlish innocence, oily overalls tend to exclude sophistication ... often I have wished I could put them all on together – just to say, 'how dare you think any of these is me. But also, see, I can be all of them'.

(Williamson, 1986, p.91)

Williamson suggests that we can choose the image that we present to others. She assumes that we have a choice, and that we know other people will understand our choices. In different cultures, these clothes, for example, would be interpreted in very different ways.

How does this develop our understanding of identity? Considering the claim that identity involves how I see myself and how others see me has led to some suggestions about how this takes place. First, we have to be able to imagine ourselves, to reflect on who we are and how we appear to others. Second, we do this through symbolizing, through producing images and visualizing ourselves. The ability to visualize ourselves and to represent ourselves gives us some degree of agency, although the repertoire of symbols upon which we can draw is always limited by the particular culture which we inhabit, as illustrated in the quotation from Williamson. This approach to the notion of identity puts more emphasis on the control which individuals have, rather than the constraints which they experience.

SUMMARY

- In constructing identities we imagine ourselves.
- We do this by visualizing ourselves, thinking in symbols.

In addressing the question about how identities are formed we have focused on the processes which are involved in constructing an identity within the individual; what happens in the social situation is left out. What else do we need to know? What happens when people present themselves to others, in everyday interaction?

3.2 Everyday interaction

Erving Goffman, the sociologist whose work has been very influential in sociology and social psychology, focused on analysis of everyday interaction, conversations and encounters. How do we communicate with others? Goffman suggested that how we present ourselves to others was rather like acting out a part in a play where the scripts are already written. In the work which we discuss here he refers to roles not to identities, but his focus on the detail of everyday interaction is also useful in exploring how we understand the identities of others and how we present ourselves. He based his work on a theatrical metaphor. He states in his book *The Presentation of Self in Everyday Life* (1959) that his perspective on the self is dramaturgical – that is, based on the idea of a performance. What we are is not given (that is, there already), it must be created. We act out in a whole range of different **roles** which are rather like parts in a play. Actors in a play cannot act out any old part and say what they like. They have to speak the lines written. However, even if the roles are written we can improvise and interpret our roles, although there are constraints.

Roles

The society into which we are born presents us with a series of roles, which are patterns of behaviour, routines and responses, like parts in a play.

Individuals, like actors, are performing for an audience. Speech, acts and gestures all require someone else to be watching or listening. The parts we play may be already written but we bring our own expectations and interpretations to these roles. We have to be convincing in order to persuade others in the audience that this is an authentic part that we are playing. For example, as a student you have to persuade your tutor that this is a serious role – that you are *really* a student. How do you do this? Perhaps you ensure that you submit your assignments on time, look earnest, carry piles of books around with you and deny any involvement in late-night party-going? The bank manager, the teacher or the doctor; each has to give a performance which convinces others of their authenticity. This is not quite the same as investing in an identity – that is, having personal commitment to an identity – but it does give us more detail about how we 'read' people and about how we get the message about 'who they are'.

A society like the contemporary UK offers a whole range of social roles which we as individuals can take up. Stop and think for a moment about the number of such positions that you occupy – in your home life, in familial relationships, at work, as a consumer, as a citizen, as a client of the welfare state or social or medical services. This involves a combination of our own expectations about a role and those of the society in which we live.

Not all of our actions in these scenarios are conscious or explicit. Sometimes we give information to other people directly. In these instances Goffman describes the public display which we intend to make when we *give* information as front stage. Appearance, clothes and gestures are crucial in the presentation of self, but sometimes the information presented may inadvertently reveal more about a person than the information directly or intentionally given. We *give off* information which we do not quite intend; for example, the nervous interview candidate who twists his fingers unintentionally is *giving off* an impression of anxiety whilst attempting to give a confident performance. The friend who is trying to look interested but who is all the while drumming her fingers and looking around may be *giving off* an impression of boredom.

The focus of Goffman's work is on everyday interactions. It offers us more ideas about answers to our first question at the beginning of Section 3: how are identities formed? His emphasis is on the social dimensions of identity and the relationship between identity, with its concern with personal investment, and roles which tells us more about the social aspects and social exchanges between people. Goffman's approach suggests that there are links between the society in which we live and the limitations offered by the roles or parts we play in that society, because the scripts have, in a sense, already been written. However, there is also scope for agency because those who play the parts can improvise and offer their own interpretation.

SUMMARY

There are some important features of Goffman's original theory which contribute to our understanding of identity and which offer more detail about how identities are presented in linking the personal and the social:

- All performances are addressed to an audience.
- Information can be given intentionally or *given off*, where we might reveal things unintentionally.

What is the source of the information which is *given off*, revealed without our consciously intending to do so? Identity relies upon a conscious, active presentation, but it might also involve thoughts and feelings about which we might not be conscious. Unintentional signs, 'slips of the tongue' are manifestations of the *unconscious* mind.

3.3 The unconscious

What mechanisms, of which we might not be consciously aware, determine our identities? Sigmund Freud's psychoanalytic theory gives us some ways in which to answer this question. One of the major contributions of Freudian psychoanalysis is his understanding of the **unconscious**, an idea which has passed into everyday language in Western societies through popular culture, the advertising industry and through psychoanalytically inspired practices like therapy. Think about the language in problem pages or used on television in the personal confession programmes on daytime TV.

Unconscious
The unconscious mind is the repository of repressed feelings and desires – often from childhood. These feelings can emerge, for example, in dreams. They can influence the choices we make in later life.

STANLEY WAS DEEPLY DISAPPOINTED WHEN, HIGH IN THE TIBETAN MOUNTAINS, HE FINALLY FOUND HIS TRUE SELF.

You may be familiar with the idea of *Freudian slips*, when the word we actually say is not the word we intended, which reveal something about our hidden desires. There may be occasions on which you have said one thing when you meant another and what you have said has been embarrassing or humorous. I can think of an example in a handwritten essay where the student wrote 'of coffee' instead of 'of course', suggesting that it might have been time for a break! Another wrote 'sexy' instead of 'sexist' in an essay on gender, which might indicate other preoccupations in the unconscious mind rather than feminist critiques of social institutions. Freud argued that these slips, jokes and dreams can reveal our 'true' feelings.

The unconscious is separate from the conscious mind and has its own rules and its own language. Freud argued, based on case studies of people he had analysed, that through early development children repress all their anti-social needs and wants, all the things a child is not allowed to do or to have. This repressed material enters the unconscious and, although it cannot be directly accessed by the conscious mind, is revealed in dreams or slips of the tongue (see Bocock, 1983). Who we are is not given in advance, we are not born with an identity, but it emerges in a number of different forms through a series of identifications which combine and emerge in an infinite number of forms so there is never one fixed, coherent identity but several in play.

You will recall that in the definition of identity in Section 1.1 it was suggested that we have to identify with an identity – that is, actively engage with a position. It is not enough to be classified by someone else, we have to take it up ourselves; for example, identify with a political party or a social movement or with enthusiasts for a type of music. **Identification** is a term often associated with psychoanalysis. Identification does not just involve copying; it involves taking that identity *into* yourself. Freud focused on male children and suggests that the little boy is especially interested in his father, although he loves his mother. He wants to grow up like his father and to take his place.

Identification
The psychological process of association between oneself and something else (originally someone else).

Psychoanalysis is one of the social theories which is organized around a concern with sex, sexuality and gender. In Freud's approach, children are seen as having sexual desires of a diverse kind. Some of these desires are repressed into the unconscious. Freud argued that the most important psychological drive is sexuality. By sexuality he meant a broad category of pleasure-seeking desires which are experienced even by newborn babies, who, for example, derive pleasure from sucking. If a child's needs are met in infancy, the child is more likely to develop into an adult with a positive outlook on life, whereas the child whose needs are not met will grow up with a pessimistic, negative disposition.

Not only did Freud argue that children were sexual but also that the most significant aspect of development was psycho-sexual. Identification with the parent of the same sex was vital for the satisfactory development of the child into adulthood. This has implications for our exploration of identity. Freud's focus on the unconscious adds to our understanding of the processes at work in the formation of identities. It suggests that we bring childhood experiences, even those about which we are not conscious, to the decisions we make as adults. This might suggest that we have limited control over the identities which we take up. They may be determined by this early childhood experience. However, Freud argues that we may be able to exercise more agency through coming to an understanding of those things which we have repressed into our unconscious minds from childhood experience, notably through therapy which can help us to understand ourselves.

SUMMARY

The importance of psychoanalytic theory for our investigation of identity can be summarized as follows:

- The identity positions which we take up may be the result of unconscious feelings which we may try to rationalize but which we do not know for sure.

- Many aspects of identity derive from childhood experience so that identity is constructed by the past as well as through the present.

- Identity is not fixed and unchanging, but the result of a series of conflicts and of different identifications.

- Both gender and sexuality are important to our understanding of identity. Our sense of who we are is most significantly linked to our awareness of our identities as women or as men.

Structure and agency in Section 3

Section 3 has focused on the question of how identities are formed and some of the processes which are involved when people take up identities and present these to other people. As we have seen, identity presents a link between the personal – that is, individuals taking up identities – and the social – that is, the social situations in which people find themselves, including social roles, everyday interactions with others and the language which we use. These accounts of identity formation offer different emphases on the role of individuals in shaping their own identities. How do these accounts address our second question:

How much control do we have in shaping our own identities?

Table 1.1 illustrates how each of the approaches discussed in Section 3 addresses this question. Each involves an interrelationship between agency and structure, but some offer more scope for agency.

TABLE 1.1

	Agency	Structure
Mead	Visualization, symbolization, imagination of individuals. We have autonomy in imagining ourselves	We have to use existing language and symbols
Goffman	Negotiation of roles; we can interpret the parts we play	The parts or scripts have already been written for the roles we play
Freud	Individuals can come to understand their childhood experience and shape their own identities. Identities are never completely fixed	Social forces can operate through the unconscious, which shapes our identities

4 LINKING THE PERSONAL AND THE SOCIAL

Identity presents the interface between the personal – what is going on inside our heads, how we as individuals feel about who we are – and the social – the societies in which we live and the social, cultural and economic factors which shape experience and make it possible for people to take up some identities and render others inaccessible or impossible. In this section, we look at other views of how identities are formed, continuing to address our first question, but shifting the emphasis on to the social aspect of the identity equation, so that we can begin to consider the third question about uncertainty and about how identities change. In order to explore the possibility that there might be some uncertainties about who we are in the contemporary UK, we need to look in more detail at the relationship between changing social structures and changing identities.

4.1 Hey you! Who me? Interpellation

What happens when individuals take up a particular identity position? You will recall that in the earlier discussion in Section 3.1 we considered the importance of symbolization and the ways in which human beings can imagine themselves occupying a particular identity. What is actually happening when we imagine ourselves as the successful candidate, the streetwise teenager or the sporting hero? Why do some identities 'work' so that we are drawn into them?

One important attempt to resolve the problem of where the individual stands in relation to socially constructed and even determined identity positions was developed by Louis Althusser who argued that when people are recruited into identity positions they are **interpellated** or hailed (Althusser, 1971).

Interpellation
A process whereby people recognize themselves in a particular identity and think 'that's me'.

It works like this. Imagine that you are walking down the street and someone calls out your name. You stop, turn round and think 'that's me, they're calling me'. Althusser argued that this is how we come to feel that an identity is the one which fits us – as a member of a religious community, as a New Labour voter, as a lad, as a mother, as a 'new man', as a European. The process is one of recognition, of looking at yourself and thinking 'that's me'! Advertising offers plenty of opportunities to think about how this works. Let me show

FIGURE 1.2 Domestic bliss: the appeal of home life (when 'gay' had a different meaning)

FIGURE 1.3 Women in the workplace: the independent mother

you an example of how some women, as mothers, might have felt 'yes that's me' in the 1950s and more recently. In the 1950s, women's magazines encouraged women, who might have worked outside the home during the wartime, to return to their domestic duties. Women were actively recruited into being housewives and mothers. And some might have felt that was the sort of mother they wanted to be, and that they fitted this identity. Women's magazines at this time sought to both promote this notion of motherhood and to enable their readers to identify with it (see Figure 1.2).

Such promotions were used in the 1950s to encourage women back into the home and into domesticity. This example illustrates a maternal identity at a particular moment in history. By 1999 a rather different maternal identity was being presented and, if the figures for women's participation in the labour market and the sale of women's magazines are to be believed, this is an identity which had purchase at this time (see Figure 1.3). In 1999, mothers might have been more likely to be 'hailed' by the pregnant woman in the workplace than by images of domestic bliss. Advertisements in women's magazines at this time plug into mothers' concerns with juggling paid work and child care.

Advertisements present us with commodities which are promoted as part of a lifestyle. Consumers can purchase symbols of the identities that they want to possess.

Can you think of examples of such advertisements which seek to interpellate the consumer in particular ways? Those for cars, for example? What sort of associations are you expected to make? Would buying a particular model of car make you seem successful, sexy, modern?

Next time you see advertisements on television or in newspapers or magazines, think about the identities which you are being invited to adopt by association.

SUMMARY

- Interpellation links the individual to the social.
- It may work consciously or unconsciously.

The work of social scientists which has been considered so far has given us more information about the processes whereby identities are formed. Some of the views discussed focused on the individual and on the details of social interaction rather than the broader picture of social structures which might constrain us. Althusser's work sought to link the individual and the social and to show how some social structures work to recruit people into identities. What can social science tell us about the ways in which these aspects of society shape our identities? What are these social structures? Are some more important than others? Are they changing?

4.2 Social structures: concepts and explanations

At this point, I am going to shift the emphasis from personal identity in the context of everyday situations to some of the social structures, such as occupation, nation, and gender, which I suggested in Section 2 were significant influences on identity. How do social scientists explain these structures? I picked out work, gender and nation, ethnicity and place as being useful examples. Each of the remaining chapters of this book focuses on one of these aspects of identity but they are introduced here to signpost what follows and to offer some preliminary discussion of the concepts which are used.

One of the ways in which social scientists have attempted to explain work-based identities is to relate them to class. Social **class** is used by social scientists as a means of classifying the economic and social divisions of a society. Different economic systems create social class groupings, which involve some degree of inequality. Chapter 3 offers a fuller discussion of different analyses of class, but it is included here as an important factor influencing the life chances and identities of those who share a class position. The *unequal* distribution of material resources is a key feature of class division.

Class
Class is a large grouping of people who share common economic interests, experiences and lifestyles.

Another source of inequality can be found in **gender** relations (gender and identity are discussed in more detail in Chapter 2). There are areas of the labour market and of domestic work, including unpaid caring work within the home, which are seen as 'men's work' or 'women's work'. In industrial societies, paid work is exchanged for remuneration and is hence more valued and has higher status than unpaid domestic work or caring work. The former has been seen as masculine and the latter as feminine. This has been enacted in most Western societies through the notion of a male breadwinner which is primary to a man's identity, whereas women's work has been seen as an extension of their roles as wives and mothers and thus as a secondary activity.

Gender
Gender describes the systematic structuring of certain behaviour and practices which are associated with women or with men in particular societies.

This indicates the importance of gender as part of the organization of a society and not just a part of each individual's experience. It is part of the

Culture
The culture of a society is its shared meanings, values and practices. Culture provides us with some of the categories and means of organizing ideas through which we make sense of our lives.

culture of a society. Assumptions about what is appropriate for women and for men can shape and influence our identities and the scope which we have for deciding both 'who we are' and 'who we want to be'.

National identity is an important part of the culture of a society. Think back to the example of the passport, in Section 2. It highlighted the importance of place, of where we come from and of institutional constructions of citizenship. The passport was proof of British citizenship but obscured gender and ethnic differences. Rights of citizenship can provide people with either considerable freedom or with restraint. Not only were women not accorded the same voting rights as men in the UK until 1928, but other rights, for example to welfare benefits, have depended on gender. The rights conferred by citizenship are often gender-related. In the UK, rights to civil citizenship have depended on gender because historically the main criterion for citizenship has been independence, based mainly on economic status. Carole Pateman argues that:

> men, but not women, have been seen as possessing the capacities required of 'individuals', 'workers' and citizens' through the dichotomy breadwinner/housewife and the masculine meaning of independence. A 'worker' became a man who has an economically dependent wife to take care of his daily needs and look after his home and children ...
>
> (Pateman, 1992, p.228)

The purpose of this example about gendered citizenship here is to illustrate the importance of gender in the construction of identities like those of the worker and the citizen, and to stress the importance of these different interrelated aspects of social organization.

SUMMARY

- The organization of society is important in shaping our identities.
- Class, gender, ethnicity and place are important dimensions of identity.
- These factors illustrate the tension between the individual and the social and between the individual's control or agency and that of social structures.

In Section 3 we briefly examined some of the explanations and concepts which social science offers in response to the two questions posed at the start: How are identities formed? How much control can we exercise over the construction of our identities? The discussion in Section 4 focused on the relationship between individuals and social structures. Changing social structures – for example, changing gender roles, patterns of employment, changing class and ethnic composition of the UK – might mean different identities are becoming available and others are disappearing. What sort of social changes have taken place in the last 50 years? In the next section we look more carefully at the changing times.

5 WHO ARE WE?

● ●

Why are we interested in identity at this point in history? Identity is certainly something of interest to academics, as illustrated by the number of books and even whole courses organized around the subject, but why should this be the case at this moment in time? Could current concerns about identity be a reflection of broad social and cultural uncertainties produced by rapid social change?

Stop and think for a moment about some of the differences between your own life and that of your parents or grandparents. What social changes might these experiences represent? What are the differences, in terms of family, marriage, divorce, parenting, work – paid and unpaid?

One of the most significant changes in the post-war period has been the move away from heavy manufacturing industry, for example steel production, ship manufacturing and coal-mining, and the increase in service sector work. Evidence shows that in the 1950s only 21 per cent of married women were in paid employment (EOC, 1981). Now the vast majority of women, married and unmarried, are in paid work or seeking work, albeit often part-time work on short-term contracts (*Social Trends*, 1998).

Whereas in the 1950s and 1960s 90 per cent of people in the UK married at least once in their lives, in 1999 the figure is down to 70 per cent with nearly half of those who marry predicted to divorce. This is very different from the number of divorces prior to the 1969 Divorce Reform Act, when the proportion was 4 per cent. In the late 1990s more people married late if they did marry, at an average age of 28 rather than 21 as was the case in the 1950s. The number of births to never-married single mothers was the fastest growing family group in the UK in 1999.

Of course there are continuities; children have to be born and to be looked after, but how and by whom? What does it mean to be a mother or a father in the twenty-first century? Is it very different from the experience of our grandparents' generation? Should mothers or fathers stay at home to look after young children, should parents pay for child care or should the state or employers provide nurseries? Even those things which we might have thought to be immutable, rooted in biological certainty, have been challenged – for example, through the use of IVF (in-vitro fertilization), a reproductive technology which enabled Liz Buttle, a 60-year-old grandmother, to give birth in 1998. New technologies appear to challenge certainties and the constraints of biology, opening up questions about 'who we are' in situations where we might have thought there was no question. All of these social changes, economic, social and technological, present questions about identity. How do we construct ourselves, for example as parents or as workers, when society's expectations are changing and new technologies create new, hitherto unthought of, possibilities? The sociologist, Anthony Giddens, has argued (1991) that these questions are a feature of contemporary life in the West. Giddens maintains that identities become both more uncertain and more diverse in a rapidly changing globalized culture.

SUMMARY

- Social changes taking place at global and personal levels can produce uncertainties in relation to who we are and our place in the world.
- Change is characterized by uncertainties and insecurities as well as by diversity and opportunities for the formation of new identities.

5.1   Is there a crisis?

Kobena Mercer, the cultural critic, argues that 'Identity only becomes an issue when it is in crisis' (Mercer, 1990). Is it 'in crisis?' There is evidence that this may be the case, for example in the ethnic and national conflicts across the world. Michael Ignatieff (1993) argues that one explanation of current concern with identity is that it is a useful explanatory concept providing a means of exploring conflict in the global context, such as in Yugoslavia, in Rwanda, in parts of the former USSR and in Ireland. Identity matters. People have a strong personal investment in political and ethnic identities, even to the extent of being willing to die for them. In such contexts, crisis might be the appropriate word.

On which other occasions have you encountered the word 'crisis', for example in the news media? The term is also employed in media constructions of social change within the UK, for example in relation to familial relations such as the increase in divorce, lone parenting and teenage pregnancies which have been identified as a 'crisis in the family' and linked to the 'crisis in masculinity', manifest in boys' underachievement at school, which is discussed in Chapter 2, or in deviant behaviour by young men (Mooney et al., 2000). Such examples may involve overstatement and a failure to address the complexities of the situations in which people find themselves. Uncertainty is not only characterized by crises. It also offers opportunities and greater diversity.

In the remainder of this chapter we are going to look at some examples of questions which involve situations where changes lead us to explore the issue of who we are and what we can now be. Uncertainty is not a new historical phenomenon but it is given different expression at different times. Have the goalposts been moved, or, perhaps more appropriately, are we now expected to play by different rules and wear a new strip?

SUMMARY

- Contemporary concerns with identity have been described as crises.
- There are also opportunities offered by the changes which are taking place.
- There are continuities as well as changes.

What are the particular uncertainties about identity at this point in history? A possible starting-point for finding out how uncertainties are expressed is to ask someone whose own life has changed.

6 WHAT DO YOU DO?

● ●

When we meet someone for the first time we are quite likely to ask them what they do in order to find out more about 'who they are'. A whole set of associated ideas about the person's identity may follow. The following extract is by John Greaves. John worked at the coal-face at Goldthorpe pit, South Yorkshire, for 20 years. For social scientists this is a particular form of evidence. It gives us information from a personal point of view. Here, in a piece of writing produced at a 'Return to Learn' course, run by the trade union UNISON and the Worker's Educational Association for unemployed miners, John describes the contrast between the mining village of Goldthorpe before 1984 and in 1997, 13 years after the pit was closed down.

ACTIVITY 1.2

Read the extract and think about these questions:

What does this autobiographical piece of writing tell us about identity?

How does John identify with the community and place in which he lived and worked?

How much control do you think John is able to exercise over the identities which he might want to adopt?

How important are social divisions like class and gender in the formation of those identities?

What are the uncertainties expressed here?

FIGURE 1.4   South Yorkshire miners

John Greaves: 'The walk to work'

Pre-1984

Woken at 4 am by a twin belled wind up alarm clock, placed out of arms' reach. Boil the kettle while having a wash and brush up. Fill a flask, snatch a quick cup of tea before making off for the day shift at Goldthorpe Colliery. Flask in pocket, acme snap tin under my arm I make my way along Furlong Road, which is busy with similar looking men travelling to their work ... The odd pair of bicycles would creak past, no matter where you worked everyone said good morning or something of the like when passing. Passing the Jungle Club at five to five the odd light would still be burning, with a customer or two still putting the world to rights, or maybe they were piloting a round the clock drinking licence. Crossing the railway bridge on the sound of diesel locomotive pulling coal wagons away from the pit. Turning into Goldthorpe's Main Street just as the five o'clock buzzer at Hickleton Colliery was sounding. Three out of Goldthorpe's five butchers' shops would have been swept and swilled down, and the owners inside cutting and slicing ready for the day's trading. All three newsagents were brightly lit, with placards outside promising news hot off the press. By far most popular was Barry's, he had lost his right arm up to the shoulder as a young man. But an artist when it came to folding newspapers, or distributing chewing gum, snuff or cigarettes. All ... would soon be discussing Saturday's match, or who would win the 3.30 at Doncaster, while Barry struggled on manfully with his task. Once served, onward towards the Pit Lane with the mouth watering smell of fresh baked bread drifting from Mr Brown's Bakers shop past all the well kept shop fronts, then reaching the Goldthorpe Hotel, which was also taking part in the open all hours scheme. Into the Pit Lane, a long concrete road with a swing park, football pitches and rugby pitches on the left and, on the right an allotment site with a shanty town of huts and greenhouses, a few with smoking chimneys. The first stop in the pit yard was the time office ... Then making a move for the pit head baths, this was where the transformation took place from normal human being into a coal miner. Off with jeans and tee shirt and on with bright orange overalls, helmet, knee pads and steel toe capped boots. Fill a large plastic bottle with drinking water before going into the hot acid smelling area known as the lamp cabin. On with a cap lamp and battery and out the

FIGURE 1.5 The National Coal Board recruits for a job with a future (below). This advertisement appeared in a football programme, October 1961 (left)

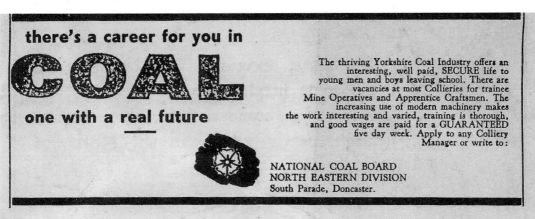

other side for a breath of fresh air, before being searched for smoking materials. Boarding the paddy train along with another 120 men to be lowered down the tunnel known as the drift, to where we worked in the black water sodden seam, that was called by people locally 'The Sludge'. Everybody was happy, hard worked but happy.

The NCB recruiting posters used to say 'A Job for Life'.

1997

Woken by a noisy milk float at 4.10 am, boiled the kettle, made a cup of tea. No need for the flask these days, and the wash and brush up seems less important. Set off for a walk, into Furlong Road towards Goldthorpe, not a soul in sight, not a house light on. Then a sign of life, a postman whistles by on his regulation Royal Mail bicycle on his way to Goldthorpe small sorting office, again I am alone. Reaching the Jungle Club at five to five, paint flaking, all in darkness no more all night sitting, too many empty pockets. Crossing the railway bridge no longer the sound of locomotives pulling coal wagons. Looking over into the cutting is a depressing sight, rails that once shone now rusting, grass growing over the once well maintained sleepers and ballast. Landing on Goldthorpe's main street at five o'clock the buzzer does not sound anymore, Hickleton Colliery no longer exists. No butchers sweeping and swilling, only one newsagent open. 'Mick's News' has retired, the shop has been extended,

FIGURE 1.6 Demolition of a colliery, South Yorkshire

brightened but lacks customers. Walking towards the Pit Land passing boarded up shops that once thrived, no longer the smell of fresh baked bread. It seems the only new traders are second hand dealers. Reaching the Goldthorpe Hotel all in darkness, silent. Turning into the pit lane to find grass growing out of every crack and joint in the concrete road. What happened to the dozens of lorries and their drivers, that used to travel this way? The pavement that was once trodden by hundreds of men a day has been lost to the grass verge. Passing the swing park, seats broken the rocking horse on its side dead! Both the football and rugger pitches look in good condition, the council took them over. The shanty town on the allotment site is thriving, perhaps looked after by people in search of the 'good life'. Into the pit yard, no time office, no canteen, no pit head baths. Just odd bits of rubble left of what was the life blood of the local community. Going down to what was the mouth of the drift, all that's left there is a steel pipe coming up from the ground, to drain away gas from underground workings. It stands like a monument to all the men who worked there, and to some who lost their lives there.

The NCB recruiting poster used to say 'A Job for Life'.

Source: John Greaves

C O M M E N T

Although John does not use the word identity, his account focuses on his sense of who he is, especially as a member of a community located within a specific *place*. In the pre-1984 period, John made sense of himself by being part of a community with a *collective identity*. Pre-1984, John was interpellated by that collective identity. By 1997 he had lost that identification.

Post-1997, his identity is fragmented and uncertain. His account tells us that this personal sense of who we are is closely tied to having a shared position linked to work (in particular, to paid work), community and place. John has lost the identity of being part of a coal-mining community which has gone with the closure of the pits. He describes economic and material changes and his regret, not only for loss of financial security, but also for the loss of a sense of belonging and the symbols with which it was associated. There is nostalgia for past security and an ambivalence about the present. What is most striking about the reconstruction of the past is the importance of the material basis of identity and its links here with paid work.

Remember the question posed in Section 5, about the extent to which there might be greater uncertainty about identity at this historical moment. An area of life which seemed to offer certainty ('a job for life'), with a clearly defined identity and sense of belonging, no longer does so. This change in economic structure and in employment forces individuals to redefine themselves. It indicates that identities are not secure but fluid and that they are constantly being re-created and redefined. The concept of identity is used here to link how people feel inside and social and material changes around them. But the extract only gives us a feel for the situation from one person's perspective. We need more and different types of evidence. Chapter 3 will look at another kind of evidence, namely quantitative, statistical evidence, that describes some of these economic changes.

The dilemma presented in this first-person narrative tells us more about the process of identity formation and about which factors might be important. What are the important dimensions of identity here? Remember the aspects of social structure which we addressed in Section 4.2. The *unequal* distribution of material resources as a feature of class division illustrated in John Greaves's account highlights the impact of structural economic change, in the form of the closure of coal-mines, on individuals' life chances and perceptions of who they are. Whilst most social scientists accept that economic changes, especially since the Second World War, have affected class relations, the impact of class on identity is debated. Class is one factor which influences identity. In John's example, although class and work-based identity may seem particularly important, other social structures also impact on the individual's experience. Coal-mining was, and is, where it still exists in the UK, a predominantly male activity with a whole string of associations about the male breadwinner and a particular brand of masculinity linked to hard physical labour.

Thus, the personal narrative also indicated the links between *class* and *gender*, where uncertainty about employment and sources of income are paralleled by uncertainty about gendered identity, notably that of the male breadwinner. Significantly higher numbers of women are in paid employment in the late 1990s than in the 1950s, although women's pay is still only 75 per cent of men's (*Social Trends*, 1999). All of these material changes have an impact on how women and men see themselves and offer structural constraints within which people have to negotiate their identities.

SUMMARY

- A first-person narrative account offers one sort of evidence of the link between the personal and the social in the formation of identities.

- The work we do is an important factor influencing the identities which we can take up.

- This example indicates the influence of structural factors, including class and gender.

- The areas of experience addressed here suggest changing times and some degree of uncertainty about 'who we are?' in relation to 'what we are'.

In the next section we turn to one of the 'everyday' questions that we might ask when we meet someone for the first time, after 'what do you do?': Where do you come from?

7 WHERE DO YOU COME FROM? RACE AND PLACE

The following poem was written by Jackie Kay who was born in Glasgow in 1961. Her mother was a white Scottish woman and her father was a black Nigerian student. She has written extensively about the subject of identity in the context of her own experience – for example, of being an adopted child, brought up in Glasgow.

ACTIVITY 1.3

Now read the poem.

SO YOU THINK I'M A MULE?

'Where do you come from?'
'I'm from Glasgow.'
'Glasgow?'
'Uh huh. Glasgow.'
The white face hesitates
the eyebrows raise
the mouth opens
then snaps shut
incredulous
yet too polite to say outright
liar
she tries another manoeuvre
'And you parents?'
'Glasgow and Fife.'
'Oh?'
'Yes. Oh?'
Snookered she wonders where she should go
from here –
'Ah, but you're not pure'
'Pure? Pure what.
'Pure white? Ugh. What a plight
Pure? Sure I'm pure
I'm rare ...'
'Well, that's not exactly what I mean,
I mean ... you're a mulatto, just look at ...'
'Listen. My original father was Nigerian
to help with your confusion
But hold on right there
If you Dare mutter mulatto

hover around hybrid
hobble on half-caste
and intellectualize on the
'mixed race problem'
I have to tell you:
take your beady eyes offa my skin;
don't concern yourself with
the 'dialectics of mixtures';
don't pull that strange blood crap
on me Great White Mother.
Say, I'm no mating of a
she-ass and a stallion
no half of this and half of that
to put it plainly purely
I am Black
My blood flows evenly, powerfully
and when they shout 'Nigger'
and you shout 'Shame'
ain't nobody debating my blackness.
You see that fine African nose of mine,
my lips, my hair, You see lady
I'm not mixed up about it.
So take your questions, your interest,
your patronage. Run along.
Just leave me.
I'm going to my Black sisters
to women who nourish each other
on belonging
There's a lot of us
Black women struggling to define
just who we are
where we belong
and if we know no home
we know one thing:
we are Black
we're at home with that.'
'Well, that's all very well, but ...'
'I know it's very well.
No But. Good bye.'

Source: Kay, 1991

What is meant by the question 'where do you come from?'?

What is the relationship being drawn between place and identity here?

What does Kay mean when she writes 'I am Black' and then 'we are Black'?

C O M M E N T

The poem indicates some of the ways in which we link identity to place and the criteria which are used for making those connections. As we saw in Section 3.2, in everyday interactions we interpret the clues which are *given* and *given off* and classify people accordingly. For many of us it is no longer possible to 'read off' identity from the same signals we might have used in the past. This poem represents a contemporary question about identity. In attempting to classify people according to where they come from we may be thrown, when there are contradictory messages given off.

In this situation it is suggested that the white woman is confused by Kay's claims to be 'from Glasgow' because she apparently feels that black people cannot be 'really' Scottish (or British). The poem describes how the white woman here ignores the replies (and Kay's Glaswegian accent presumably) and insists that to be black is to be an outsider.

The poem also highlights the way in which identity is marked by **difference**. We have already seen that people mark their identities by some symbols of difference – scarves, badges, clothes, ways of speaking. This time the difference suggests that the white woman defines Kay as an outsider, in an *unequal* relationship of 'us and them'. 'Us' includes people who are the same as us, using the criteria which we think mark us out as the same, for example being white; 'them' are marked out as different because 'they' are not the same as 'us'. This suggests that 'we British' should be a superior category to 'those foreigners'. The key point about difference in the example of the poem is that being black or white is not only a way of marking difference but is used as a means of asserting superiority. Such assertions of superiority and the attempt to exclude people on grounds of race can be described as racist.

Difference
Difference is relational. It has to be defined in relation to something else. For example, Monday is the day after Sunday and the day before Tuesday. Difference often involves oppositions which are unequal.

This poem is also about a search for certainty and disquiet about uncertainty. When 'snookered' by her earlier questions the white woman resorts to questions about 'purity'. She is seeking to locate identity in a category which we can mark off as fixed and certain. Kay's response to the misconceptions of the white woman is to deny any uncertainty on her own part. She gives voice to a collective identity which has meaning for her as an individual. She may be unclear about where she 'comes from' but is quite certain about who she is, who she wants to be and with whom she belongs. In her response Kay is offering one possible solution to the uncertainties posed by the question 'where do you come from?' in a multicultural society.

Multi-ethnicity and cultural diversity arising from the cultural differences in the contemporary UK raise a number of questions about uncertainty and diversity and about the ways in which people have the possibility, or not, of constructing their own identities. How can people respond so that they can actively engage with shaping their own identities? What kind of action is appropriate and how do we resolve the dilemmas with which we are presented? One strategy is to assert and celebrate difference as Kay does in her poem, in order to take control of her own identity. We have already seen unequal power relations, especially in the context of economic factors, as in our example of coal-mining. In this example, we see the social constraints which can operate through racist practices and ideas.

SUMMARY

- Identity is based on being the same as some people and different from others.
- Identities are constructed in relation to place.
- Difference is unequally weighted and can create some people as outsiders.
- Individuals and groups have to negotiate both the uncertainties of social change and the constraints of inequality.

Next we turn to another question which we might ask when we want to know more about someone. This time it suggests that people might have more control over their own identities.

8 WHO DO YOU WANT TO BE?

New social movements
Protest groups that challenged traditional politics and made identity a key factor in political mobilization.

It is not only through individual engagement that people seek to exercise agency and to forge new identities. The advent of **new social movements** in the West in the 1960s indicated collective endeavours to shape and give voice to new identities. These movements challenged traditional constraints and sought to celebrate a group's positive features as well as to challenge oppression. For example, the women's movement, the black civil rights movement, gay and lesbian rights movements, and the peace movement all sought actively to redefine the identities of their members. Campaigns around environmentalism, the politics of HIV and AIDS and for the rights of people with disabilities have challenged the idea that identities are fixed and cannot be reconstructed. The political projects of these group activities asserted collective identities. They also involve appeals to a certainty upon which the identities are based. For example, some gay rights activists have argued that their sexual identity is grounded in their biological make-up and is not a product of social processes. Some feminists have argued that women are intrinsically more peace-loving than men and that women have essential, female qualities which are superior to male aggression and should be celebrated as such – for example, as in the Greenham Common peace campaign.

FIGURE 1.7   Newbury Bypass protesters

FIGURE 1.8   Disability rights protestors, Whitehall, July 1994

FIGURE 1.9   Gay rights protestors campaigning for the age of consent to be lowered to 16 for gay men

One of the concerns of *new social movements* has been to make us think in different ways about traditional ideas. Through collective action the word *gay* became a more positive representation of a sexual identity. Such social movements attempt to subvert stereotypes, shape new identities and celebrate diversity.

8.1 Body projects

In contemporary society the body has become a project. People attempt to alter or improve the appearance, size and shape of their bodies in line with the their own designs. Think about the situations where this might happen: some people train at the gym or decorate their bodies with tattoos or even alter the appearance of their bodies through plastic surgery, such as face-lifts, liposuction and breast implants. Such body projects have become a feature of contemporary society, perhaps because of the consciousness people have of the inescapable reality of death: bodies age, become infirm and are subject to illness and disease. Body-building and boxing are examples of projects which challenge accepted notions of what is natural, especially when it is women who are involved in the activity. This can be seen as a form of resistance to constraining stereotypes of femininity.

ACTIVITY 1.4

Look at Figures 1.10 and 1.11.

How important are the constraints of the body and of biology here?

What do these pictures tell us about the ways in which it is possible to assert an identity through the body?

FIGURE 1.10 A woman body-builder demonstrates posing

FIGURE 1.11 The boxer Jane Couch training

COMMENT _____

Arguments about what is 'natural' and about biology have been used to justify women's exclusion from particular activities. The women in these pictures can be seen as exercising agency to develop a particular kind of body which challenges cultural stereotypes. They are challenging what is thought appropriate gender behaviour. This illustrates one of the ways in which people use the body as a site for the construction of identity. Sometimes people engage in body projects which conform to existing stereotypes, but sometimes, as here, they assert resistance and create new identities. The body itself clearly offers some restrictions on what it is possible to do, but it is often difficult to disentangle what is biological and what is cultural. This is because we represent ourselves through the body itself as well as through what we wear. Sometimes campaigning groups which seek to present more positive images of themselves and to represent their collective identities do so through reconstructing the body and its images and challenging traditional expectations.

ACTIVITY 1.5

Look at the poster in Figure 1.12.

FIGURE 1.12 Hello boys?

Without looking at the words on the poster, what is the first thing you notice?

What is the stereotype which this image is designed to subvert?

COMMENT

Age Concern used this picture of 56-year-old Pearl Read, posing in the style of Eva Herzigova in the Wonder Bra advertisements featured on hoardings across the UK in the late 1990s, to challenge the expectation that older people are unattractive and not sexually attractive. We may be more familiar with representations of young women as in, for example, the original Wonder Bra 'Hello boys' advertisement. This illustrates the importance of *representations* in the construction of identities. The most obvious in the above image is the association of sex and sexuality with provocative underwear. The item of clothing itself does not carry this meaning – it is the *association* which conveys it. In a women's changing room it would have a different meaning. Sexuality is one of the most frequent associations used in the promotion of commodities – for example, in car advertisements which include attractive and scantily dressed women. Meanings depend on the relationship between objects in the world and how we make sense of them in our heads. Words and images act as signs which express meaning but the meanings change according to the situation. This poster is a good example of the way in which symbols, often the same symbol, can be used to produce different meanings. In the original Wonder Bra advertisement, the message conveyed and the meaning of the symbol is sexual attractiveness and the promotion of the product by interpellating the would-be attractive woman purchaser. In the Age Concern poster, the pose and the look are used to symbolize a challenge to ageism and the constraints of stereotyping people according to their age.

One of the certainties which would appear to be offered by biology is that the human body declines in capabilities and attractiveness with age and eventually dies. What this poster does is to indicate the social meanings which are attached to the biological body. It presents a more complex view of ageing which suggests we as individuals might have some *control* over the process and especially the meanings associated with it.

SUMMARY

- Individuals and groups seek to challenge social expectations about identity.
- Through collective action and through individual projects people resist dominant cultural representations of identity.
- We can look in detail at how representations are produced and the role they play in the formation of identity.

9 CONCLUSION

Are we now better equipped to answer the three questions posed in the introduction?

How are identities formed?

We present ourselves to others through everyday interactions, through the way we speak and dress, marking ourselves as the same as those with whom we share an identity and different from those with whom we do not. Symbols and representations are important in the marking of difference and in both presenting ourselves to others and in visualizing or imagining who we are. We use symbols in order to make sense of ourselves in relation to the world we inhabit. This world is characterized by structures which may limit our choices, but which may also provide more opportunities.

How much constraint is exercised by social structures and how much control do we have in shaping our own identities?

Both as individuals and through collective action it is possible to redefine and reconstruct our identities. We can negotiate and interpret the roles we adopt. Through collective action it is also possible to influence the social structures which constrain us, but there are clearly restrictions and limits. The scripts of our everyday interactions are already written and at the wider level structures are deeply embedded in contemporary culture, economy and society. Identity formation continues to illustrate the interrelationship between structure and agency.

Is there more uncertainty about 'who we are' in the contemporary UK?

There have been changes in our lives, in the domestic arena, in the workplace, in our communities and at the level of the nation and its place in the world. Some of these changes have been translated into questions of identity, for example in concerns about how people cope with change. Change has also created new opportunities for redefining ourselves, at home and in the workplace and as members of different ethnicities and nations within the UK. There is both uncertainty and diversity. Identity is a particularly useful concept for explaining how people cope with change and uncertainty and the opportunities presented by diversity. Identities are fluid and changing. This, in itself, produces uncertainties.

This chapter has introduced not only some concepts and theories used by social scientists but also some of the ways in which they approach their task. We have started with *questions* and some tentative *claims*. What is happening to identities? How are they formed? Having offered some *definitions* which included the marking of difference and similarity and the link between the personal and the social, we then went on to find some *evidence*. Some of the evidence suggested that we know about the marking of difference through symbols and representation, which itself suggested *more questions* about how these symbols work. Could they work at the level of the unconscious? In order to explore further the link between the personal and the social we read an autobiographical account, another piece of evidence to which we applied some of the concepts about social structures which had been introduced earlier. This chapter has only introduced these ideas of social scientists starting with a question, seeking evidence and using concepts and theories to begin to offer an explanation. At each stage new questions emerge. The remaining chapters of this book extend this process, focusing on specific dimensions of identity. In Chapter 2 we look at something which appears to be grounded in biology, gendered identities. In Chapter 3 we focus on the economic bases of identity, and in Chapter 4, using the example of the nation, we explore further the role of culture in shaping identities. The questions which were posed at the outset in this chapter and to which we have returned will inform the rest of the book so that we can produce a more complex picture of how identities are formed, the link between the personal and the social, the tension between structure and agency, and the degree to which identities are formed at a time of uncertainty which also offers diversity and opportunity for change.

REFERENCES

Althusser, L. (1971) *Lenin and Philosophy, and Other Essays*, London, New Left Books.

Bocock, R. (1983) *Sigmund Freud*, London, Tavistock.

Equal Opportunities Commission (1981) *Annual Report*.

Giddens, A. (1991) *Modernity and Self-Identity: Self and Society in the Late Modern Age*, Cambridge, Polity.

Goffman, E. (1959) *The Presentation of Self in Everyday Life*, New York, Doubleday Anchor.

Ignatieff, M. (1993) *Blood and Belonging: Journeys into the New Nationalism*, London, Chatto and Windus.

Kay, J. (1991) *A Dangerous Knowing*, London, Sheba.

Mead, G.H. (1934) *Mind, Self and Society*, Chicago, University of Chicago Press.

Mercer, K. (1990) 'Welcome to the Jungle' in Rutherford, J. (ed.) *Identity: Community, Culture, Difference*, London, Lawrence & Wishart.

Mooney, G., Kelly, B., Goldblatt, D. and Hughes, G. (2000) DD100 *Introductory Chapter. Tales of Fear and Fascination: The Crime Problem in the Contemporary UK*, Milton Keynes, The Open University.

Pateman, C. (1992) 'The patriarchal welfare state' in McDowell, L. and Pringle, R. (eds) *Defining Women*, Cambridge, Polity.

Social Trends, London, HMSO (annual).

Sarup, M. (1996) *Identity, Culture and the Postmodern World*, Edinburgh, Edinburgh University Press.

Williamson, J. (1986) *Consuming Passions*, London, Marion Boyars.

FURTHER READING

Richard Jenkins (1996) *Social Identity*, London, Routledge. This is an accessible introduction to debates about social identity which draws mainly on the disciplines of sociology and anthropology. It offers a well-illustrated discussion which elaborates the theories introduced in this chapter.

Madan Sarup (1996) *Identity, Culture and the Postmodern World*, Edinburgh, Edinburgh University Press. This book integrates ethnical material on identity with personal narrative about events in the author's autobiography. He provides accessible coverage of a range of approaches to identity with a focus on culture and representation.

Identity and gender

Jennifer Gove and Stuart Watt

chapter 2

Contents

1 INTRODUCTION

In this chapter, we are going to focus on one important dimension of identity, gender, and look at two significant claims about the way identity is constructed. First, we are going to investigate Kath Woodward's claim in the previous chapter, that gender identities are shaped by many different factors: individual and collective; biological and social. We are going to suggest that gender illuminates the complex multiple origins of identity very clearly, because it allows us to explore our capacity for agency, and the social and biological structures that constrain our freedom to choose our gender identities.

In practice, biological and social differences between women and men are sufficiently important that we often use different words to describe them. This distinction between **sex** and **gender** is sometimes a very useful tool in the social sciences, because it allows us to concentrate on social differences between women and men, without worrying too much about biological differences. The problem with this distinction is that often biological and social influences are very tangled. Woodward's passport example clearly shows this tangling. Official documents do not actually use the word 'gender'; they use the word 'sex' instead, and everyone is categorized as either male or female. Many official documents, such as passports, birth certificates and death certificates, record sex explicitly.

Sex
Sex is a biological classification.
Gender
Gender includes the social attributes associated with being a woman or a man in a particular society.

Feminine and masculine
Terms which are applied to the qualities particular societies associate with women and men.

Our second claim is that the way we construct our identities is strongly influenced by a set of rather stereotypically **feminine** and **masculine** characteristics and traits that we often associate with gender categories, with women and with men. But women and men are not made from a single mould. There are many different kinds of women and men, and different traits may apply to some more than to others. Behind the apparent simplicity of two genders, there is a diversity of gender characteristics, and many different influences are at work.

All societies have ways of differentiating between women and men, and between femininity and masculinity. These differences are often expressed through stereotypical language, through words which are associated with women and with men. The activity which follows includes some examples of this kind of language.

ACTIVITY 2.1

Let's look at some of these stereotypical characteristics. Table 2.1 contains 45 different terms which might be used to describe people. Which, if any, of these words would you apply to yourself?

Reflect on the terms that you have chosen, and what they say about your identity. Do you think you are typically masculine or feminine?

TABLE 2.1 Some words that could be typical of one gender or another

tall	tender	arrogant
lucky	active	jealous
humane	proud	individualistic
tactful	modest	commanding
athletic	intuitive	unpretentious
weak	kind	passive
benevolent	decisive	conventional
assertive	unfriendly	strong
irresponsible	tidy	co-operative
perceptive	playful	robust
anxious	unemotional	reponsive
gentle	informal	flexible
vulnerable	calm	acute
dignified	vigorous	cheerful
crude	faithful	timid

Your responses will vary according to how you see yourself and the culture you are from. However, as we have seen, how you see yourself is only one part of identity. Now let's look more at the social side of identity, and consider how these different traits might be categorized by society as a whole, so that some are associated with men and others with women.

ACTIVITY 2.2

Look through the list of character descriptions in Table 2.1 again. For each one, write down whether you think it is thought to be typical of men or women in general, or neither, in your culture today.

COMMENT

Table 2.2 shows a gendered categorization of these traits, based on a small survey which we carried out. This shows how they can be regarded as culturally typical of women and of men. Look again at your answers to Activities 2.1 and 2.2 in the light of this possible classification. There is clearly scope for disagreement here. Look specifically for differences between this classification and your answers, and think about why these differences might exist.

TABLE 2.2 Typically feminine and typically masculine characteristics

Feminine characteristics	Masculine characteristics	Neutral characteristics
anxious	active	acute
co-operative	arrogant	benevolent
faithful	assertive	calm
gentle	athletic	cheerful
humane	commanding	conventional
intuitive	crude	dignified
kind	decisive	flexible
passive	individualistic	informal
perceptive	irresponsible	jealous
responsible	proud	lucky
tactful	robust	modest
tender	strong	playful
tidy	tall	unfriendly
timid	unemotional	unpretentious
vulnerable	vigorous	weak

Categorizations like these reveal some aspects of how society and culture describe, and prescribe, gender-appropriate behaviours, qualities, and characteristics. These categories are not only the product of everyday exchanges; they can even be used in psychological testing, to classify and to measure the way we see ourselves.

How then can we use categorization to explore our two claims – the multiple sources of gender identity and the role of gender stereotypes?

In this chapter, we begin by looking at one theory of identity formation: *self-categorization theory*. Then, in Section 3, we will look at the development of gender identity in children, and in Section 4 we will look at the effects of gender identity on school performance.

SUMMARY

- Gender is a key dimension of identity.
- Gender identity is influenced by individual and collective and social and biological factors.
- Gender identities are often associated with stereotypically feminine and masculine traits.

2 GENDER IDENTITY AND SELF-CATEGORIZATION

Where does identity, and gender identity in particular, actually come from? We are going to focus on one account of the origins of gender identity by Turner and his colleagues (Turner *et al.*, 1987) called *self-categorization theory*. This explanation is rather like Althusser's concept of *interpellation*, described by Woodward in Chapter 1, Section 4.1.

In Althusser's account of identity, people are interpellated, or hailed, when they see a representation of a category and think, 'yes, that's me'. Look at Figure 1.2 in Section 3.4 of Chapter 1. Quite literally, we are encouraged to *identify* with representations like this. These representations connect individuals to groups, and by becoming members of groups individuals take on new identities. The word 'identify' is telling: it signifies that the relationship between the individual and the representation has an emotional quality, an 'empathy', as well as a feeling of sameness. This is important to identity; it has a real feeling of personal involvement. Identity matters, at a personal level as well as a social one.

2.1 Explaining identity: self-categorization theory

Turner and his colleagues' theory claims that identity is shaped by self-categorization; by people looking at social categories, and deciding whether or not they are in a category. If they consider themselves a member of a category, that category becomes part of their identity. The explanation given by Turner's self-categorization theory works like this:

1 We see people as members of social categories.

2 We also see ourselves as members of social categories.

3 We take on identities appropriate to the social categories with which we identify.

Identity, then, includes people's notions of who they are, of what kind of people they are, and their relationships with others. It is therefore closely related to the *groups* – the social categories – that they see themselves as belonging to. So, for example, if Chris has an identity as a woman, this means that (a) she sees people divided into gender categories of women and men, and (b) she sees herself more as a member of the category of women.

Turner and his colleagues claim that similarity and difference influence self-categorization, and therefore identity. In effect, people are more likely to identify with a category they are similar to, compared with a category that is more different. The more different the person in the image is from you, the less likely you are to identify with it. Women are more likely to identify with the image in Figure 1.2 in Chapter 1 than men are.

So far, we have said very little about how gender categories actually work. We know that we refer to them using words like 'women' and 'men'. And to some extent we know what is going on inside them: we know there are traditionally feminine and masculine characteristics associated with each category, although these may vary between times and cultures. But to understand Turner's explanation properly, we need to be clearer about how we decide which gender category someone is in? This is central to steps 1 and 2 of Turner's explanation.

Let's look at an example of this happening in practice. What happens when a child is born? What category, *male* or *female*, will be written on their birth certificate? And what factors, biological or social, influence this categorization?

2.2 Gender categories: 'Is it a boy, or is it a girl?'

Lord Melchett   The whisper on the underground grapevine, ma'am, is that Lord Blackadder is spending all his time with a young boy in his service.

Queen Elizabeth I   Oh. Do you think he'd spend more time with me if I was a boy?

Lord Melchett   Surely not, ma'am.

Nursie   You almost were a boy, my little cherry pip.

Queen Elizabeth I   What?

Nursie   Yeah. Out you popped from your mummy's tumkin and everyone shouted, 'It's a boy! It's a boy!' And then someone said 'But it hasn't got a winkle!' And then I said, 'A boy without a winkle! God be praised – it's a miracle! A boy without a winkle!' And then Sir Thomas More pointed out that a boy without a winkle is a girl, and everyone was really disappointed.

Lord Melchett   Yes, well, you see he was a very perceptive man, Sir Thomas More.

Source: Elton and Curtis, 1998, pp.123–4

In the days of Queen Elizabeth I, practically the only significant factor which decided at birth whether the child was a girl or boy was the appearance of their genitalia – in effect, whether or not they had a 'winkle'. In this respect little has changed since then. But is this really enough to define someone's gender? For Freud, as discussed in Chapter 1, Section 3.3, it was certainly very important. A child's psycho-sexual development depends on identifying with others of the same sex – and in this, Freud's explanation of gender relates to a child's self-categorization. And Freud, like Sir Thomas More, thought that girls' gender was significantly formed by the *absence* of a penis. This is illustrative of unequal power relations between the genders; the anatomical evidence is being used to reinforce a distinction that matters to society.

There is another problem with using anatomical evidence to define gender. In society, we usually wear clothes that hide a lot of our bodies. While for the most part we do not reveal our genitalia to people we meet casually, we usually have little problem deciding whether they are men or women. Because people usually wear clothes which present gender cues, social evidence is complicated by bodily evidence. Furthermore, because of the clothes, we can't usually see the anatomical evidence to help us tell the difference between women and men. So are there any other, more reliable, sources of evidence that we could use instead, to tell the difference between the gender categories?

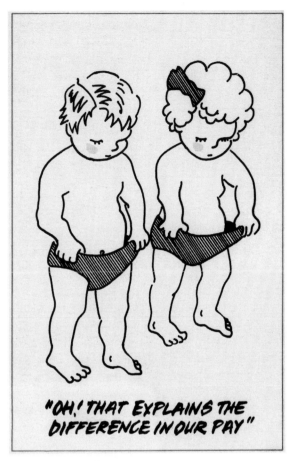

"OH! THAT EXPLAINS THE DIFFERENCE IN OUR PAY"

© LEEDSpostcards

A second possible way to tell the difference between men and women is to use genetic evidence. Inside every cell in the human body is a number of long strings of the chemical DNA, called chromosomes. Of these, two, called the X and Y chromosomes, are called sex chromosomes. Generally speaking, humans either have two X chromosomes (and develop physically as women) or one X and one Y chromosome (and develop physically as men). So instead of checking for physical differences, we could use the genetic difference between women and men to define sex.

But there are problems with using genetic evidence to decide who should go into which category, just as there was with the bodily anatomical evidence. This time, it is the occasionally blurred boundary between the categories that shows the problem most clearly. Very rarely, people have more than two sex chromosomes; for example, people may have two Xs and one Y. But because females usually have two Xs, and males an X and a Y, these genetic intermediates could be categorized either way. Physically, too, they may have a mixture of bodily characteristics that makes categorization less certain than usual.

One solution to this problem is to define the categories more precisely. For example, Connell (1987) gives the example of the International Olympic Committee which decided simply to *define* all people with an intermediate pattern of chromosomes as men, so regardless of physical appearance they would not be allowed to participate in women's events. To categorize people at the Olympic Games, genetic tests are used, rather than physical checks. But this definition was made by a committee to maintain the status of the Games. The decision to use genetic evidence to define the categorization was made by a controlling social group. This has created problems for the individuals concerned, who suddenly find themselves re-categorized. Once again, biology does not give us a complete explanation of gender difference. Neither bodily nor genetic differences work all the time. Is there anywhere else we can look for a more certain account of the gender difference?

Another possibility is to argue that the difference between boys and girls is socially constructed. One hint of this is in the birth certificate itself. After birth, it is the birth certificate itself that defines sex, at least in the UK. Although the sex written on the certificate is based on biological evidence about our bodies at birth, and this evidence is assessed by a (presumably expert) doctor before being written into the formal certificate, the birth certificate then takes on a life of its own. It is this document that counts for

FIGURE 2.1 Official proof that we exist?

getting passports, citizenship, marriage, and so on; the original bodily evidence then becomes more or less irrelevant. To get a passport, or to get married, you do not need to display your genitalia.

So wherever we look we find that social and biological influences are tangled. At the bodily level, and at the genetic level, there are social influences at work, and at the social level there are biological influences at work. Many factors contribute to defining gender: the way we dress and cut our hair, the genetic information inside our cells, and the form of our bodies. No single set of these defines, unambiguously, whether we are men or women.

Something else about the gender categories may have struck you. Why are there two categories? Why are people not all in one gender category? After all, the differences between men and women are pretty small compared with the similarities between them. This is a tricky issue, which we will come back to in Section 3, but remember what Woodward said in the previous chapter: *identity is marked by difference*. Categories, such as gender categories, can reflect an *unequal* relationship of *us* (those inside the category) and *them* (those outside, in a different category). The differences between us as individuals are reduced compared with the larger differences between *us* and *them*. In other words, without difference, there could not be such a thing as identity; without a *them* there could never be an *us*. Categories, such as the gender categories that we have investigated, are organized into systems which make 'us and them' possible.

2.3 Are we free to change our gender identity?

In current UK law, even if bodily evidence is changed, there is no way for a person's legal sex to be changed accordingly. This is because, in the UK, someone's legal sex is defined by the sex assigned at birth. What is commonly called a 'sex change' operation (more correctly known as 'gender reassignment') does not affect a person's legal sex, and they can still only legally marry someone of the opposite sex to that on their birth certificate. Although someone may adopt a new gender by changing their clothes, their behaviour, and even their body, the birth certificate constrains their use of the new gender. The birth certificate takes the uncertainties of gender, and hides them as far as the law is concerned. In the UK, people are not completely free to choose their gender identity.

There are two stories we can tell about what defines gender categories. According to the first story, there is an *essence* to a category, which things have if they are in the category, and do not have if they are not in the category. Having a penis, or having a Y chromosome, are good examples of this kind of essence to the category 'male'. This story about categories is

Essentialist
This viewpoint regards, say, having a Y chromosome as essential to being a male and reduces gender to one factor. An account of identity in general and gender identity in particular which reduces gender to possession of a single characteristic or essence.

called **essentialist**, because it regards, say, having a Y chromosome, as essential to being male and reduces gender to one factor. All other gender characteristics, such as those categorized as masculine in Table 2.2 above, would simply be consequences of having this essence. However, as we discussed earlier, there do not seem to be any essential characteristics, at either the bodily, genetic, or social level, that unambiguously decide gender category membership.

In the second story, there are no clear criteria as to whether or not something is in the category. Instead, the category is rather fuzzy. Although most of the cases may be really clear, there are a few unclear cases around the edges. This story about categories is non-essentialist, simply because there is no essence to the category; many factors contribute to the gender categories. As we have seen, gender categories seem to be non-essentialist in character.

Because essentialist categories are clear, they tend to remain fixed. Fuzzy categories, on the other hand, can and do drift a bit, so what it is to be a woman, or man, may vary as times and cultures change.

2.4 Gender stereotypes

Essentialist categories have important consequences. Essences are all or nothing – you are either in the category or outside it, but there is no in-between. With non-essentialist categories, you can be more or less in the category. There is a lot more room for diversity. People can be more or less typical representatives of the gender categories that they belong to. There are many kinds of men and women – typical men and atypical men, and similarly typical women and atypical women, rather than just men and women – although what counts as typical will vary between cultures. Typical men, for example, might have most of the characteristics that we would expect of 'men in general'. Atypical men have rather fewer of the characteristics we might expect; they might, for example, be bored by sport on television, not have a car to wash on Sunday afternoons, or they might enjoy doing the washing up.

Stereotype
A simplified representation of the most typical characteristics associated with a category.

Typicality, as we have cast it, looks a bit like masculinity or femininity. Is this the case? Where do these 'typical' features that we associate with gender categories come from? Look back at Figure 1.2 in Chapter 1. This image is interesting because it represents a stereotype. A **stereotype** is a simplified, and possibly exaggerated, representation of the most common typical characteristics associated with a category. Despite the fact that it may be biased, it often, although not always, has a grain of truth (look at your responses to Activities 2.1 and 2.2 if you are not convinced). Stereotypes are usually either positively or negatively biased, although different people may hold very differently valued stereotypes. Positive stereotypes, such as the image of the pregnant woman in the workplace in Figure 1.3 in the previous chapter, often encourage identification. Negative stereotypes, on the other hand, are associated with prejudice. The word 'prejudice' means judging people *before* you have met them, and this is exactly how both positive and negative stereotypes work, although they may continue to influence our perceptions afterwards for good and for ill.

This link with identification is important, as it suggests that stereotypes – particularly positive stereotypes – are linked with identity. In fact, Turner and his colleagues' explanation makes a clear claim: that positive stereotypes are generally linked to, and defined by, the *in-group* (the one you are a member of) and negative stereotypes tend to be linked to, and defined by, the *out-group* (the one which is different, which you are not a member of). Because of this difference between the groups, the positive and negative stereotypes tend to reflect, and even reinforce, Woodward's unequal relationship of *us and them*.

2.5 Masculinities and femininities

Stereotypes do not just shape the way we perceive other people, they also shape the way we behave. People are active players in the development and construction of their own identities. People can, within limits, change themselves to fit their understanding and views of gender. As part of this, people often adopt gender-typical behaviour to form and fit with the identities that they construct. Identity is not just something we achieve, nor something that is just thrust upon us; it has elements of both.

Looking back at Activities 2.1 and 2.2, you should now find that categorization makes makes more sense of stereotypes. The characteristics in Tables 2.1 and 2.2 are illustrative of the gender stereotypes. But where did these characteristics come from?

We selected these characteristics by running a small experiment. We put together a big pool of possible traits, and presented it to a panel of judges. These judges were asked to rate each characteristic by how strongly gender-linked it was. We treated the judges not as giving a correct categorization, but simply as a window on to one particular culture – in this case, the UK in 1999. Other cultures are rather different, and times change, so there may be some significant differences between different cultures' interpretations of the traits in Table 2.1, and about what is considered gender-appropriate in a culture. Sandra Bem conducted a study in the USA in the 1970s (Bem, 1974). Her findings suggested that there were distinct and recognizable characteristics associated with femininity and masculinity in the USA at the time. There have been some shifts. Today, in the UK, it may be a little more acceptable for men to exhibit feminine traits, but in other ways not so much has changed.

Something else might have struck you about the character descriptions in Tables 2.1 and 2.2; the descriptions are not equally valued within a culture, although the characteristics that are most valued will vary between cultures.

For example, men are described as individualistic, assertive, and athletic, women as intuitive, perceptive, and tactful. Bem recognized this issue: in her study she interpreted the feminine and masculine, not as opposites, but as different dimensions, as shown in Figure 2.2. Bem considered it possible to be both masculine and feminine at the same time (she called this type of person 'androgynous'), or to be neither masculine nor feminine (she called this 'undifferentiated'). She wanted to abandon the common-sense opposition of feminine and masculine, and offer freedom for a greater diversity of masculinities and femininities, allowing both women and men to be free agents, able to take on the valued characteristics.

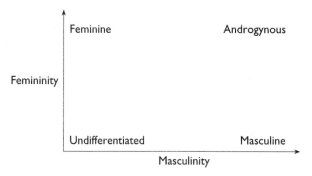

FIGURE 2.2   Dimensions of femininity and masculinity in Bem's Sex Role Inventory
Source: Turner, 1995, Figure 6, p.17

SUMMARY

- Turner and his colleagues use *self-categorization theory* as an account of identity, an account that links with Althusser's notion of interpellation.
- Self-categorization theory suggests that identity is shaped by the categories with which we label ourselves and identify.
- Gender categories show biological, social, and possibly even genetic, factors at work, but no clear single influence dominates.
- Gender categories are also associated with stereotypes, which may be either positive or negative, and which can reinforce the relationship of 'us and them'.

So far, we have looked in considerable detail at adults' gender categories, and at how they might work to shape the construction of our gender identities. In Section 3 we will explore how children construct and take on identities as they develop.

3 GENDER IDENTITY AND GENDER DEVELOPMENT

In this section we are going to look at where we come from in terms of childhood experience and the development of gender identities in childhood. We have already learned that gender identity involves the construction and use of gender categories. Children's gender categories are at first rather simplistic; but, as we shall see, children refine their categories so that they become more reliable and useful for their social lives. Studying the development of gender identity in children reveals that this is a story of a search for certainty. In Section 2 we discovered that self-categorization is a necessary part of developing a gender identity. In exploring the formation of gender identity in children it would therefore be sensible to ask questions about children's construction and use of gender categories.

We look at four key questions in this section:

- At what age do children display behaviour that suggests they are using gender categories?

- At what age can children categorize themselves (and others) as belonging to a gender category, and what does this categorization mean to them?

- Are young children's gender categories different from those of adults, and if so in what ways?

- How are gender identities maintained in later childhood?

What evidence exists about children's use of gender categories? Children's preference for particular toys is some of the earliest behaviour indicating a categorization of masculine and feminine. Preferences, behaviours or traits that

FIGURE 2.3   Some toys are considered to be appropriate for boys and others for girls

Gender-appropriate
Preferences, behaviours or traits deemed to be suitable or proper with regard to masculinity and femininity in a particular culture.

mirror the views of one's society about what is masculine and what is feminine are termed **gender-appropriate**. Opting for gender-appropriate toys (masculine toys such as trucks, toolkits, and construction kits if one is a boy and feminine toys such as dolls, tea-sets, and domestic items if a girl) can usually be seen by 2 years of age. There is evidence that from 3 or 4 years, children are able to categorize toys as suitable for boys or girls, and knowledge of the gender-appropriateness of toys strongly influences preferences.

Our second question asked about children's ability to categorize themselves appropriately. Some researchers believe that consistent gender labelling is a particularly important milestone. Most children can categorize themselves appropriately and consistently as a boy or girl at some time between 2 and 3 years of age. Durkin (1995) describes this as a gradual process:

> ... the child slowly becomes aware that he or she is a member of a particular sex. At first, this knowledge constitutes little more than a label for the child, equivalent to a personal name. The child begins to discover which other individuals fall into the same category, and elaborates his or her gender labels to include terms such as man, woman, boy, girl. But knowledge is not perfect.
>
> (Durkin, 1995, p.180)

There is evidence that some important gender-appropriate behaviours result from the child's ability to categorize themselves as a boy or girl. Such behaviours include having a greater preference for same-gender peers. However, some gender-appropriate behaviours such as toy preference, as we have seen, occur before this milestone is typically reached. Once children are able to categorize themselves and others appropriately, they can draw upon (and build upon) their previously acquired knowledge to refine their construction of gender categories, and further develop their own sense of gender identity.

So from quite an early age children are able to categorize themselves as male or female. Perhaps this is early evidence of the formation of gender identity. What, though, does the label that children initially apply to themselves actually mean to them? What did Durkin (in the quotation above) mean when he noted that children's knowledge 'is not perfect'? The answer to these questions depends upon evidence relating to our third question about the development of gender identity. This question asked whether the gender categories used by young children differed from those of adults. Learning more about the characteristics of children's gender categories can tell us more about the sorts of gender identity they are forming.

Research has found that gender categories typically constructed by young children under about 5 years of age have particular and distinct characteristics (Kolhberg, 1966). The evidence for this is revealed through mistakes that children make. They may, for example, suggest that girls can become uncles, and boys become aunts. In addition to misunderstandings about the stability of gender over time, children are often also fooled by context. If outward appearances change, if, for example, a man dresses in woman's clothing, or if a man engages in activities considered to be typically feminine, then children may consider such a man to have changed into a woman.

Think back to Section 2 in which we discussed how categories can be constructed in different ways. What may the structure of young children's gender categories be like, such that they result in misunderstandings about gender?

Young children's gender categories are highly stereotyped. This can lead to assured predictions of an individual's preferences based upon knowledge of their gender, and the kinds of activities that they may typically engage in. Children develop such rigid gender categories in their search for certainty about gender. These categories are essentialist, having a simple in-group and out-group distinction that children use for understanding masculinity and femininity, and for defining their own gender identity. However, because the categories they use are inflexible, this leads them to make mistakes about gender. Given these distinctive characteristics of young children's gender categories, we can describe children as being *naïvely certain* about gender.

How might the construction of children's gender categories lead them to believe that gender may not be stable throughout life? Although a few people may change their gender identity, as adults we need a sophisticated understanding of this, rather than a naïve belief that when surface characteristics change (such as clothes and make-up) so does gender. Take a look at the quotation below:

Johnny (age 4½) I'm going to be an airplane builder when I grow up.

Jimmy (age 4) When I grow up, I'll be a mommy.

Johnny No, you can't be a mommy. You have to be a daddy.

Jimmy No, I'm going to be a mommy.

Johnny No, you're not a girl, you can't be a mommy.

Jimmy Yes, I can.

Source: Kohlberg, 1966, p.95

Jimmy, although of an age where he can presumably label himself as a boy, believes that he can be a mommy when he grows up. The current construction of his own gender identity does not restrict him to remaining the same gender throughout life. Why might this be? Research conducted by Bem (1989), described in Box 2.1, illustrates that young children look for certainty in gender categories that they construct using *social* and *cultural* characteristics. Bem's study reveals that young children's categories are less influenced by *biological* knowledge, and this, claims Bem, is principally because they simply do not have this knowledge.

> ### BOX 2.1 — What are young children's gender categories made of?
>
> In an experimental study, Bem (1989) found that only about half of 3, 4, and early 5-year-olds were able to draw upon biological knowledge (genitalia) in deciding whether pictures of nude toddlers were boys or girls. Most of the children who were successfully able to identify boys and girls from biological cues were subsequently able to categorize the same children consistently as boys or girls when they were shown pictures of them in clothes and with hairstyles characteristically associated with the opposite gender. In other words, most children who were able to categorize gender on the basis of biological cues were not swayed in their judgements by the contradictory gender-cues presented through surface appearances. Most of those children who could not correctly identify boys and girls from seeing their genitalia were more likely to decide the gender of the same child in subsequent pictures on the basis of appearance.

So early gender categorization is particularly dependent upon social and cultural experiences. Perhaps this can help us to understand why young children make mistakes about the stability and constancy of gender, and why their gender categories are defined in highly stereotypical ways. As adults, we know that just because someone changes appearance from one gender to another (for a fancy dress party, for example), or just because they engage in activities that are considered to be typically appropriate to the opposite gender, they nevertheless remain the gender that they are. This is because our understanding of gender embodies both biological and social knowledge – our understanding of gender is complex and sophisticated. We understand (unlike young children) that changing our gender identity takes more than changing our outward appearance or the activities that we do. In addition, we also understand that just because someone prefers woodwork, football, and beer over needlework, netball, and wine, it does not necessarily mean that person is a man. This is because we are aware that the links between our stereotypes do not correspond neatly to being a man or a woman; there is indeed diversity with regard to gender in our society. However, if we were made to place a bet about someone's gender given particular characteristics, we might draw upon our stereotypical knowledge in doing so; but stereotypes cannot be relied upon, and as adults we know this.

Multiple gender identities Masculinities and femininities, rather than one masculine and one feminine type. In any society there is a whole range of ways in which femininity and masculinity can be expressed.

Gradually, children's culturally defined gender categories are supplemented with biological knowledge. Children from about 5 years of age onwards learn that their own and others' gender identity generally remains the same across time and across contexts. This is a profound development in the gradual construction of gender identity. As the gender categories that children develop become more reliable, they also become more flexible and are no longer essentialist. Children learn that there are **multiple gender identities,** masculinities and femininities, rather than one masculine and one feminine type. Children are still certain about gender, just as we generally are as adults;

but this is now because, like adults' categories, their categories become more reliable and adaptive.

Although gender categories become more flexible, they continue to work as powerful social tools. The gender categories used in the construction of gender identity are actively maintained and re-constructed throughout our lives. But, as our fourth question asks, how does this come about? Francis (1997, 1998) has conducted some interesting research with school children, that examines the construction and maintenance of their gender identities. This research is described in Box 2.2.

BOX 2.2   **Gender identity and gender maintenance**

Francis (1997, 1998) asked primary school children (aged 7 to 11 years) to engage in some pretend role play. The groups of children were asked to choose between play situations of a hospital, hotel, or school, and they had to choose the roles that they were going to play from a set provided. Francis observed the children's play and examined their talk. In choosing their roles, boys took the high-status positions of doctor, manager and head teacher slightly more often than girls. Those boys taking high-status positions used their role to exert domination and power far more often than did girls.

The gender roles the boys took on and constructed could be described as 'typically masculine' and those of the girls as 'typically feminine'. Particularly when playing in mixed groups, the children constructed the gender roles as oppositional to each other. In general, Francis found that the girls took on sensible, selfless, mature, and facilitating behaviours, and boys took on silly, selfish, immature, and demanding behaviours. Such gender-typical behaviours correspond to previous research with school children which has consistently found girls at school to be diligent, sensible and quiet and boys to be rowdy, disruptive, and preoccupied with violence. Francis interprets the children's constructions of oppositional gender roles to be part of a process of identity maintenance.

Adoption of typical gender identities generated situations in the role play in which the girls (typically feminine) behaviours, such as willingly accepting low-status roles, and facilitating the role play with their sensible suggestions, supported the boys' (typically masculine) behaviours of taking up high-status roles and behaving in a demanding and selfish way. Francis notes how the girls' adoption of such feminine positions is simply demonstrative of socially appropriate feminine behaviour, which she describes as exemplifying a 'properly female' identity.

Francis is careful to point out that these gender-appropriate identities and behaviours were not taken up by all children; instead, they were fluid, and some children challenged or ignored them. Francis suggests that children work quite hard in constructing and maintaining their gender identities; but it also highlights that the behaviours typical of masculine and feminine roles are not binding, and that there is opportunity for diversity. Why are gender categories and gender identities not fixed? One reason, as Francis points out, is that gender constructions are only one part of our identities, alongside ethnicity and social class, for example. Sometimes the influences of these other factors may reinforce those of gender; at other times they may outweigh them, and this affords diversity. Because many factors interact in the construction of identity, there can be no single masculinity or femininity; there must instead be a diversity of masculinities and femininities.

This section has discussed the typical pattern of gender identity development and has shown that gender is crucial to identity and our understanding of who we are. But just as there is diversity in terms of masculinity and femininity, there is diversity too in children's acquisition of gender identity. Children have different experiences and develop at different rates. It is also important to note that research takes place at a particular time, and in a particular place, so the story of the typical may also be culturally biased.

SUMMARY

- Children's developing understanding of gender can be described as a search for certainty.

- Young children make mistakes about gender illustrating their rigidity and their naïve certainty regarding gender.

- As children's knowledge of gender grows in complexity, basic biological knowledge is added to their social–cultural understanding.

- Research by Francis illustrating girls' 'sensible-selfless' and boys' 'silly-selfish' behaviour demonstrates how gender identities are constructed and maintained.

- Children's knowledge of gender in relation to their own identity and that of others develops both in terms of flexibility (in that they can accommodate diversity) and in reliability.

- Masculine and feminine identities are not fixed, partly because identities are multidimensional. Diversity arises through the existence of masculinities and femininities.

We are going to continue to follow the story of what is typical through investigating how constructions and perceptions of gender identities may affect experience of school and subsequently performance at school. We will explore the claim that performance in exams may to a certain extent be dependent upon gender, both in terms of one's own identity, and in terms of how schooling as a social process deals with masculinity and femininity.

4 GENDER AND ACADEMIC ACHIEVEMENT

● ●

ACTIVITY 2.3

What do you recall about being at school? Note down your thoughts. The following questions may help you:

What did you do in the playground? If you played games, what were these?

What did you do in physical education lessons?

Did you participate in any out-of-school activities? What were these?

What were your favourite school subjects?

Which subjects were you good at and which were you bad at?

Can you see any patterns or themes in your answers?

Do you think that any of the activities you can remember doing were related to your gender?

COMMENT

People's experience of school differs greatly. Your reflections on gender differences in your school years may depend upon how long ago your schooling was, and the sort of school you went to. You may have attended a single-sex school; or perhaps, in your coeducational school, boys and girls were separated for some subjects, such as physical education. Your school's curriculum might have dictated different activities for boys and girls. Perhaps you can remember whether girls' or boys' names were called first when the register was taken, or whether where you sat in class depended upon gender. You may remember the sorts of subject you opted for, and how good you and others were at different subjects.

There are clear patterns in the subjects that boys and girls take and do well at in school. For a long time boys were found to perform better than girls in science exams, and girls have outperformed boys in English. Such general trends cannot necessarily explain the performance of individuals. Indeed, the significant diversity in performance across gender should also be recognized. However, the strong statistical patterns in performance relating to gender that do exist are worthy of social scientific investigation.

4.1 'Boys performing badly'

In 1944, the Butler Education Act introduced a three-tiered system of schooling in England and Wales. Based upon results in the eleven-plus examination, pupils could attend either a grammar school, a technical school (though there were few of these), or a secondary modern school. More grammar school places were made available for boys. This practice was justified on the basis of boys' 'later maturity'. Class became an issue of concern relating to this tripartite system, since the middle classes were disproportionately represented in grammar schools; but in general gender issues were not addressed. It was not until feminists raised the issue of gender inequalities in schooling during the 1960s and 1970s that gender, and particularly lack of opportunities for girls, linked up with political and research agendas. Until recently, concern has generally been focused on female underachievement. However, the latest trends, reported widely through the media, have shown girls out-achieving boys in subjects traditionally considered as 'male', such as mathematics, science, and technology-based subjects, and the gap in achievement for English increasing. The statistics made the headlines, some of which can be seen in Figure 2.4.

Girls outclassing boys

The Guardian, 26 November 1997, p.1

Now boys' results give 'cause for concern'

TES, 5 December 1997, p.4

Girls really are better than boys – official

The Observer, 4 January 1998, p.1

Boys performing badly

The Observer, 4 January 1998, p.13

FIGURE 2.4
Newspaper headlines relating to changing patterns in examination results

Why do you think there has been such concern about boys' underachievement, but no such *moral panic* when girls were underachieving in mathematics and sciences in the 1950s and 1960s?

The poor performance of boys caused widespread concern which was unprecedented in relation to previous debates about gender and school achievement, which suggests a profound concern with boys' underachievement. The situation was declared a 'crisis' and the government requested action to address the problem from each education authority. It is not only Britain that has been experiencing this trend in the underachievement of boys compared with girls. Similar patterns can be found across a number of developed countries (Murphy and Elwood, 1998), as can the consequent alarm.

Let us have a look at the figures for ourselves. Figure 2.5 displays the percentage of 16-year-old girls and boys in England achieving GCSE A*–C grades in (a) five or more subjects, (b) English, (c) Maths, (d) Science.

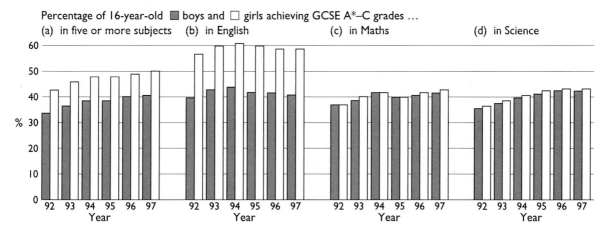

FIGURE 2.5 Bar chart of girls' and boys' GCSE results
Source: *The Observer*, 4 January 1998

Chart (a) shows that overall percentages for both boys and girls are increasing; but that more girls obtain five or more GCSE passes at grades A*–C than boys. Chart (b) shows that girls consistently outperform boys in English. Chart (c) shows girls beginning to achieve higher grades than boys in mathematics. Chart (d) shows that girls out-achieve boys in science (though not to the extent that they do in English). Where the differences look small, remember that they represent very large numbers of students.

A careful examination of detailed government figures reveals that the 'crisis' is not as straightforward as often presented. For example, treating all science results together hides issues regarding the proportions of girls and boys entered for the different sorts of science exams that exist. These different sorts of exams (separate science subjects, single-science, and double-science) have different status, and statistics of results for GCSEs in England suggest that girls are more likely to be entered for the less prestigious awards. This shows that the way the statistics are reported affects the story that is told. However, rather than explore these intricacies in more detail here (important though they are), we will turn our attention to reflecting upon *why* differences in performance may exist. We will consider whether differences are *natural*, to do with the biology of being male or female; and whether experiences of, and interactions with, social structures can account for differences found. In our consideration of social and cultural influences, we will also discuss the construction and assessment of the tests and exams upon which performance is based.

4.2 Exploring the origins of performance differences

Cognitive tests are designed to measure the ability to reason perceptually, mathematically, and linguistically. Results of such tests show that, although there is a great deal of similarity in the areas in which males and females both achieve, in general males do better on some sorts of tasks and females do better on others. Some examples of these tasks can be seen in Figure 2.6. The premise of such research is that differences found between large samples of males and females are *natural* and innate. Such research can be considered to be a search for certainty in relation to gender differences.

Researchers investigating the biology and physiology of brain structure and function suggest that cognitive specialization of males and females (for example, women tend to do better on verbal tests and men on spatial tests) may be due to organizational differences in the brain, or influences of early sex hormones (Kimura, 1992). However, it is very difficult to claim that cognitive testing can give a measure of *natural* ability, since lifestyle factors (the different experiences of men and women) can never really be excluded.

Criticisms of the tests themselves also challenge the claim that men and women have distinct problem-solving abilities. As Birke points out, 'Tests may measure only a very limited range of appropriate skills; verbal skills, for example, include a wider range of abilities, such as reading, and may depend upon other abilities, such as reasoning' (1992, p.99). In addition, interpretation of the results can be problematic. Many test results show no or little difference between the performance of males and females, highlighting instead similarities in distributions of achievement, and such results often go unreported.

Birke raises a further concern about the relationship that is drawn between performance on cognitive tests and 'natural' biological predispositions. She writes, 'It is ... a strange kind of biology – for these theories portray the differences as somehow etched into a fixed kind of brain. Yet surely the human brain is anything but fixed: on the contrary, it shows amazing capacities for learning and memory' (1992, p.100). Birke questions the pursuit of certainty, and reliance on ideas of fixed differences between men and women. The differences found may result from a complex **interaction** between biology and social–cultural experiences: biological processes are responsive to environmental influences and vice versa. None the less, the view that cognitive strengths and weaknesses of men and women are 'determined' by an unalterable biology is pervasive.

Interaction
Biological processes are responsive to environmental influences and vice versa.

Problem-Solving Tasks Favoring Women

Women tend to perform better than men on tests of perceptual speed, in which subjects must rapidly identify matching items– for example, pairing the house on the far left with its twin:

In addition, women remember whether an object, or a series of objects, has been displaced:

On some tests of ideational fluency, for example, those in which subjects must list objects that are the same color, and on tests of verbal fluency, in which participants must list words that begin with the same letter, women also outperform men:

L _ _ _	Limp, Livery, Love, Laser, Liquid, Low, Like, Lag, Live Lug, Light, Lift, Liver, Lime, Leg, Load, Lap, Lucid ...

Women do better on precision manual tasks–that is, those involving fine-motor coordination–such as placing the pegs in holes on a board:

And women do better than men on mathematical calculation tests:

77	$14 \times 3 - 17 + 52$
43	$2(15+3) + 12 - \dfrac{15}{3}$

Problem-Solving Tasks Favoring Men

Men tend to perform better than women on certain spatial tasks. They do well on tests that involve mentally rotating an object or manipulating it in some fashion, such as imagining turning this three-dimensional object

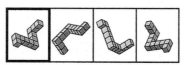

or determining where the holes punched in a folded piece of paper will fall when the paper is unfolded:

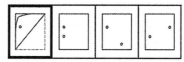

Men also are more accurate than women in target-directed motor skills, such as guiding or intercepting projectiles:

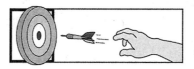

They do better on disembedding tests, in which they have to find a simple shape, such as the one on the left, once it is hidden within a more complex figure:

And men tend to do better than women on tests of mathematical reasoning:

1,100	If only 60 percent of seedlings will survive, how many must be planted to obtain 660 trees?

FIGURE 2.6

Cognitive testing: problem-solving tasks favouring women and men

Source: Kimura, 1992, pp.82 and 83

Some of the criticisms that have been brought against cognitive tests can also be applied to school tests that have generated the recent 'crisis'. Birke raised the issue that tests sometimes do not actually measure what they are supposed to measure, or that they may only measure a highly restricted range of abilities. Psychologists describe this as a concern with the *validity* of the tests. This type of argument has also been made by feminist educationalists and applied to school testing. Ideas surrounding performance have been broadened and realized in the wider criteria for testing implemented through GCSE examinations; but despite the shift from testing knowledge of facts to testing the use of knowledge, tests and examinations still serve to define school achievement particularly narrowly. Another anxiety about the validity of cognitive tests was the likely, but often unacknowledged, influence of social and cultural factors. In short, perhaps boys and girls have different experiences inside and outside of school, which may explain the achievement patterns. Let us look at these experiences in more detail.

From the early 1970s, feminist studies have shown how women (in all sorts of contexts) are often considered the inferior 'Other'. Since the beginnings of formal education, women's education has been considered as secondary to men's, and the curriculum for women was shaped by beliefs about biology, the female body, and the services that women would consequently 'naturally' aspire to (Paechter, 1998). This is explored in Box 2.3.

BOX 2.3   Educating the Other

Paechter (1998) in her book *Educating the Other* notes that in the nineteenth century there was:

> ... a concern to protect adolescent girls from 'mental overstrain' and it was believed that 'over-educated' women would be unable to breast-feed ... At the same time, it was this assumed future role of wife, and in particular, mother, that to a large extent shaped nineteenth and twentieth century girls' education.

(Paechter, 1998, p.12)

Further, she notes that at the beginning of the twentieth century:

> ... a girl might spend half of the time in her last year on domestic subjects. This of course led to the exclusion of other studies; boys were usually taught elementary arithmetic while the girls did needlework ... Both the elementary and secondary curricula for girls emphasised an ideology of service; this persists up to the present day, inscribed in the practices not only of food and textile technology ... but also of business subjects ... Summerfield (1987) argues that schools still teach girls that their main objective is preparation for a caring role, both in the home and at work, so girls are encouraged to regard themselves as secondary, servicing, Other to men.

(Paecher, 1998, p.13)

Education has had, and still has, a particular purpose for girls that is different from and inferior to that for boys. It claims that the different experiences of girls and boys shape identities in specific ways. Of course, there have been many changes both inside and outside school since the beginnings of formal education.

Can you think of any changes with regard to gender identity and gender roles within educational establishments since you were at school?

If you have only recently left school, try to think of changes since you started school.

Changes in social structures may contribute to shifts in attitudes, and the construction of new, though perhaps still distinctive, masculine and feminine identities at school. Although the research evidence is not conclusive, economic and labour market changes may be playing some part in shaping the attitudes and self-perceptions of particular groups of boys and girls and influencing their behaviour in school. There may therefore be at least an indirect effect on performance.

Whilst there is much debate about whether there are increasing opportunities for women to take higher status managerial positions, or whether the *glass ceiling* is just as resilient as ever, the proportion of women in such jobs has increased. At the same time, uncertainty has been experienced by many men in regions where traditional apprenticeships and other routes for boys into the labour market have been in sharp decline. A number of research studies have suggested that this rather dramatic labour market shift has perpetuated a particular youth sub-culture – 'the macho lads', who, with no potential for achievement in terms of working-class male craftsmanship, do not identify with schooling. They seek alternative anti-school values and adopt 'laddish' attitudes and behaviour (Mac an Ghaill, 1994). This may be a result of societal changes challenging traditional gender identities. The newspaper comment and discussion headlines shown in Figure 2.7 suggest that it is the attitudes, values and identities of these boys that underpin poor achievement patterns.

Other evidence suggests that the notion of achieving academically is now broadly linked with femininity, and that this is shunned by some boys in the construction and expression of their masculine identities. The current experiences of boys suggest that it is 'uncool' to be seen to be a high achiever and that one must at all costs avoid gaining the identity of a 'boffin'. In fact, cultivating an identity that will be accepted by peers in school may require the careful adoption of particular behaviours:

> I get a bit of stick myself because I really like English. Sometimes I don't bother answering or asking questions in class because I will worry that my friends will take the mickey out of me for being teacher's pet.
>
> (Daniel, aged 13, quoted in *The Guardian*, 6 January 1998, p.6)

> In the year above me there's a boy who wears five merit badges and he gets stick off everyone. I've got two, but I only wear one.
>
> (Sam, aged 13, quoted in *The Observer*, 4 January 1998, p.13)

How to turn the new lads into new men
The Guardian, *Education*, 13 January 1998, pp.2–3

Learning gender gap reveals redundant male
The Observer, 4 January 1998, p.19

A bad way to educate boys
The Independent, *Education+*, 3 April 1997, p.8

Problems that arise when boys will be lads
The Guardian, 6 January 1998, p.6

Boys turned off by homework
TES Scotland, 23 January 1998, p.3

FIGURE 2.7   *Newspaper discussion headlines relating achievement and male identities*

Particular aspects of typically masculine and typically feminine identities relate to specific school-based activities and to achievement. One recent and much publicized example is that of reading, now commonly considered to be a feminine interest, and more often recognized as part of feminine rather than masculine identities. Note Daniel's reflection on his peers' reaction to his enjoyment of English, as reported in the above quotation from *The Guardian*.

Whilst there is much concern about boys' poor levels of literacy, and the increasing gender gap evident in English examinations, it is important to consider the implications of such gender-related patterns of achievement.

Although girls are excelling in English, it is an English that focuses upon what has been described as nineteenth-century literary and literacy habits, rather than literacy in computer and communications media required in a rapidly changing world (Kress, 1998). Here we return to the issue of breadth of definitions of performance; but we should also consider the implications of gendered subject preferences. It is currently the subjects that are disproportionally taken by males at the higher levels, such as computer studies,

FIGURE 2.8 The relationship between educational attainment and work is not a straightforward one

engineering, and physical sciences, that are highly valued in our society, and that often reap the highest financial rewards in the world of work. Kress warns that, if we ignore the growing divide between the world of school and work, then 'Girls' achievement would be rewarded by the education system; but not by the world of work' (1998, p.5). Reflections such as these indicate that the uncertainties generated by shifts in performance patterns and employment opportunities do not have straightforward implications.

4.3 Gendered identities and school performance

In Section 4.3 we will look at the construction of a social science argument, using the example of educational achievement differences. Murphy and Elwood (1998) suggest that typically masculine and typically feminine attributes are developed through interactions with parents, peers and schooling (and other such social agents) from infancy. They provide evidence suggesting that masculine and feminine attributes are differentially perceived and rewarded within the structures of our education system.

They front their research by arguing:

> The question considered in this paper is not what girls and boys can or cannot do; but what it is that girls and boys *choose* to do. What lies behind their choices and how do gendered choices influences achievement?

(Murphy and Elwood, 1998, p.95)

Notice Murphy and Elwood's focus on choices and influences on those choices. They suggest that certain factors impact on personal agency with regard to subject choice and achievement, and build up their argument by exploring a number of claims. We will use the evidence they have gathered to explore three claims that they believe provide an explanation of school performance in terms of gendered identity:

- *Claim 1:* 'Boys' and 'girls' foster different interests, attitudes, and behaviours prior to attending school, which are then perpetuated within school.

- *Claim 2:* Feminine and masculine identities are perceived in particular ways by teachers, with consequences that may impinge on achievement.

- *Claim 3:* In their school-work, 'girls' and 'boys' draw upon the different interests and skills that they have developed through their gendered experiences. However, the sorts of knowledge and style of expression produced by 'girls' and by 'boys' are often differentially rewarded. Typically masculine forms of expression are more highly rewarded in some subject areas (such as the sciences), and typically feminine forms of expression in others (such as English).

Murphy and Elwood (1998) use quotation marks around the words 'boys' and 'girls' when they want to denote reference to boys with typically masculine and girls with typically feminine interests, behaviour and traits. We have followed this convention when referring to their work.

The first claim suggests that children arrive at school with gendered interests and behaviours. On the basis of previous research, Murphy and Elwood propose that culturally-based socialization practices structure the experiences of 'girls' and 'boys', and can account for gendered identities.

Murphy and Elwood highlight how 'girls' and 'boys' develop interests in different types of play, with girls typically enjoying creative activities, and

FIGURE 2.9 Children first learn about gender-appropriate behaviour from their immediate world

boys typically enjoying constructional activities. In participating in different activities 'girls' and 'boys' consequently acquire different skills associated with those activities. Different interests are also developed with regard to discussion and reading topics that 'girls' and 'boys' enjoy and this contributes to the construction of masculine and feminine identities. Murphy and Elwood assert that, if children are familiar with the activities and topics they encounter at school, they will have confidence in pursuing them; but if the activities they encounter are at odds with their interests, they are likely to lack confidence and become alienated from their tasks. This leads 'boys' and 'girls' to make particular choices and engage with certain school activities and not with others. Murphy and Elwood (1998) focus on science classes as an example of this. 'Boys' have typically had more experience with scientific apparatus outside school contexts, and they adapt to the use of similar equipment within science lessons better than do 'girls'. 'Boys' maintain their advantage through dominating use of the equipment.

FIGURE 2.10 Do girls and boys have equal opportunities in practical science work?

Jackson (1998) also highlights how school knowledge, which as we have seen is narrowly defined, serves to engage some children and alienate others:

> This has undermined the abilities and destroyed the confidence and motivation of many working-class girls, members of ethnic and cultural minorities and some working-class boys. Many boys have felt brushed aside by the dominant definition of school knowledge – their home and community languages, their often raw but direct insights and their everyday, street knowledges have all been experienced as invalid.
>
> (Jackson, 1998, p.79)

The second claim suggests that teachers react to gendered identities as expressed within school contexts in particular ways. Teacher interventions, non-interventions, and responses may well complement the choices that children are already making. Murphy and Elwood note how lack of confidence, typically experienced by girls in relation to certain topics, '... is all too often interpreted as lack of ability' (1998, p.102). Other characteristically masculine and feminine behaviours are also interpreted by teachers with subtle but important consequences. Thinking back to the study by Francis reported in Box 2.2, you will remember that in general girls' attitudes tend to be more conforming than those of boys in school contexts. Whilst this conformity may be highly regarded by teachers, in comparison to the risky, gambling approach that some boys take to their work, it can be taken as evidence of less (or, more usually, very 'average') ability. The more unusual, less conformist approach adopted by some boys is often taken as indication of an acute brain, a 'bright spark'. Similar expectations have been found in children's and young people's self-perceptions, with boys typically overrating their abilities, whilst girls underrate theirs (Joffe and Foxman, 1988).

Murphy and Elwood suggest that the judgements that teachers make of ability can have direct implications for performance. One example provided is that, in 1994, 5 per cent more females than males were entered for the middle band of the GCSE mathematics exam (in which a C grade is the highest level awarded). More boys were entered for the higher band (which risks an unclassified grading if performance drops below grade C). Murphy and Elwood point out that this may be a consequence of teachers' *perceptions* of females' confidence in mathematics, and *judgements* made about their anxiety.

The third claim argues that particular styles, expressions, and representations of knowledge are valued in particular subjects areas, and that these correspond to masculine and feminine favoured work styles. In other words, performance is dependent upon the style of response presented, and this differentially affects 'girls' and 'boys' depending upon the subject matter.

ACTIVITY 2.4

Figures 2.11 and 2.12, reproduced from Murphy and Elwood (1998), are typical examples of drawings which children produced when asked to design a boat to go around the world, giving details of things that were important.

Look at these pictures in some detail. What differences do you see between the girl's picture and the boy's picture?

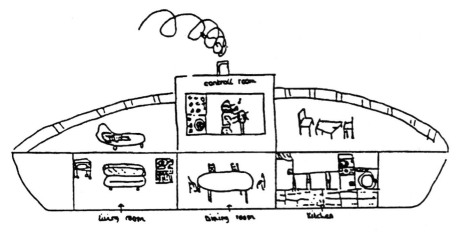

FIGURE 2.11

A typical girl's boat

Source: Murphy and Elwood, 1998, p.104

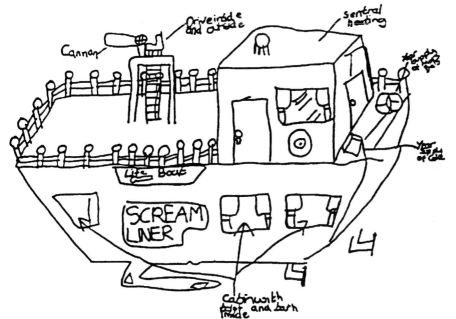

FIGURE 2.12

A typical boy's boat

Source: Murphy and Elwood, 1998, p.104

C O M M E N T

We noticed that the girl's picture in Figure 2.11 features details of the furniture and home comforts that she considers important for a trip around the world. In contrast, the boy's picture in Figure 2.12 concentrates on the design of the boat. It appears as if the children interpreted the question in very different ways. The girl attended to the details for the people who would be living on the boat, and the boy attended to the construction of the boat itself that would enable it to get around the world. The concern that 'girls' hold about human needs are typically at odds with the more context-free requirements of school science. In this scenario, if the teacher had intended the construction of the boat to be the focus of the task, then this effectively undervalues 'girls'' perceptions of the task, and generally 'boys'' work would gain higher marks.

We have already noted how the literacy styles and interests of boys and girls differ before and during, as well as outside and inside, school. The argument is made by Murphy and Elwood that the different interests, activities, and experiences of 'boys' and 'girls' affect the work done in school and lead to differences in examination performance. Although 'boys' may be very good at dealing with presenting facts, this is not what is required in English exams and they consequently tend to underachieve in this area. In contrast, 'boys'' analytical styles are rewarded within science, whereas 'girls' may not have had the experience to develop appropriate expression in this area. The work of Murphy and Elwood suggests that examination results reflect gendered identities, rather than a divergence in ability levels between 'boys' and 'girls'.

At the end of their paper, Murphy and Elwood comment on the importance of considering socio-economic backgrounds in relation to achievement. This is a crucial issue. Furthermore, not all boys are failing, and not all girls are out-achieving boys. Identity and academic achievement is not just an issue of gender; it also embodies issues of individual differences, social and economic groupings, ethnicity, and nationality.

SUMMARY

- Over the last few years there has been much media interest in the 'crisis' of boys' underachievement. Generally, boys do seem to be doing less well than girls in GCSEs; but the picture is more complex as it relates to particular groups of boys and girls, and involves many other influences, such as class and ethnicity.

- Results of cognitive testing indicate that men and women have strengths in different sorts of tasks. Although this is suggestive of *natural* innate differences, evidence suggests that social and cultural factors may account for some of the results.

- There are concerns about the validity of school examinations. School knowledge is narrowly defined and this alienates particular groups of children.

- Particular school subjects and examinations, as currently defined, may reward the ways of working and styles of expression typically adopted by girls, whilst other subjects may reward boys' typical work styles.

- There are individual differences in relation to school performance, as well as diversity between groups of boys and girls. This is partly related to the multidimensionality of identity, and the range of masculinities and femininities existing in our social world.

- Consideration of the implications of gender differences in schooling suggests that there may potentially be continuities in trends (such as the low status of 'women's work') despite important recent changes.

5 CONCLUSION

● ● ● ● ● ● ● ● ● ● ● ● ● ● ● ● ● ● ● ●

In this chapter we have investigated gender identities through looking at gender categories – how we construct and use them, and how we come to consider ourselves as gendered beings. We have found that gendered identities have repercussions for experiences at school, educational performance, and economic life chances.

We started this chapter with two claims. The first was that gender identities are shaped by many different factors. We found that biological factors (such as the forms of our bodies, or the genetic material inside them) and social factors (such as the experiences we have inside and outside schools) are not independent. Gender identity, like identity more generally, is a complex interweaving of a variety of different influences: biological factors that are affected by the environment (even if only through our cultural perceptions of biology), and social factors that are influenced through our (often rather naïve) understandings of biology. Second, we claimed that the way we construct our identities is strongly influenced by feminine and masculine characteristics associated with the gender categories, men and women. We have seen evidence that as individuals we can choose which aspects of gender identity to take up, but our choices are constrained by a variety of factors, including cultural perceptions of masculinity and femininity.

To explore the flexibility of gender categories and the diversity of gender identities we have looked at development from childhood to adulthood, and seen how developing an understanding of gender involves a search for certainty. In early childhood, gender categories are used in a fixed, often stereotypical, essentialist way, but gradually, as children learn more about their social world, gender categories become more sophisticated and flexible. This increasing flexibility accommodates a diversity of masculinities and femininities. It is clear that gender identities are not fixed; they shift and change across time and between cultures. However, evidence suggests that our identities are not something that we are completely free to choose and use exactly as we want; they are shaped by society, the culture that we live in, and our experiences and understandings. The identities of particular groups of males and females may be constrained or liberated when pitched against historical agendas and social structures, such as education and the economy. Although we may feel free to choose our identities, social and cultural factors, which include class and ethnicity as well as gender, contribute to the sorts of identities that we hold.

Murphy and Elwood's argument was studied in some detail because they made an explicit explanatory claim linking gender identities to the gendered achievement patterns seen in examination results. Their evidence suggests that particular sorts of knowledge and styles of expression are required by different school subjects, and that these subject-specific requirements differentially benefit 'boys' and 'girls'. Murphy and Elwood suggest that if school children were more aware of the different styles of expression expected in different subject areas, and were taught skills to deal with these requirements, then perhaps gendered inequalities in achievement patterns would diminish. The evidence they present is powerfully illustrative of the gradual process of identity formation and the consequences of living with gendered identities.

REFERENCES

Bem, S.L. (1974) 'The measurement of psychological androgyny', *Journal of Consulting and Clinical Psychology,* vol.42, pp.155–62.

Bem, S.L. (1989) 'Genital knowledge and gender constancy in pre-school children', *Child Development,* vol.60, pp.649–62.

Birke, L. (1992) 'In pursuit of difference: scientific studies of women and men' in Kirkup, G. and Keller, L.S (eds) *Inventing Women: Science, Technology and Gender,* Cambridge, Polity.

Connell, R.W. (1987) *Gender and Power: Society, the Person, and Sexual Politics,* Oxford, Basil Blackwell.

Durkin, K. (1995) *Developmental Social Psychology, from Infancy to Old Age,* Oxford, Blackwell.

Elton, B. and Curtis, R. (1998) *Blackadder II: Bells* in Curtis, R., Elton, B. Lloyd, J. and Atkinson, R. *BlackAdder: The Whole Damn Dynasty,* London, Michael Joseph.

Francis, B. (1997) 'Power plays: children's constructions of gender and power in role plays', *Gender and Education,* vol.9, pp.179–91.

Francis, B. (1998) 'Oppositional positions: children's construction of gender in talk and role plays based on adult occupation', *Educational Research,* vol. 40, no.1, pp.31–43.

Jackson, D. (1998) 'Breaking out of the binary trap: boys' underachievement, schooling and gender relations' in Epstein, D., Elwood, J., Hey, V. and Maw, J. (eds) *Failing Boys? Issues in Gender and Achievement,* Buckingham, Open University Press.

Joffe, L. and Foxman, D. (1988) *Attitudes and Gender Differences,* Slough, NFER/Nelson.

Kimura, D. (1992) 'Sex differences in the brain', *Scientific American,* September, pp.81–7.

Kohlberg, L. (1966) 'A cognitive-developmental analysis of children's sex-role concepts and attitudes' in Maccoby, E.E. (ed.) *The Development of Sex Differences,* Stanford, CA, Stanford University Press.

Kress, G. (1998) 'The future still belongs to boys', *The Independent (Education),* 11 June, pp.4–5.

Mac an Ghaill, M. (1994) *The Making of Men: Masculinities, Sexualities and Schooling,* Buckingham, Open University Press.

Murphy, P. and Elwood, J. (1998) 'Gendered experiences, choices and achievements – exploring the links', *Journal of Inclusive Education,* vol.2, no.2, pp.95–118.

Paechter, C. (1998) *Educating the Other: Gender, Power and Schooling,* London, The Falmer Press.

Summerfield, P. (1987) 'Cultural reproduction in the education of girls: a study of girls' secondary schooling in two Lancashire towns 1900–50' in Hunt, F. (ed.) *Lessons for Life,* Oxford, Basil Blackwell.

Turner, J.C., Hogg, M.A., Oakes, P.J., Reicher, S.D. and Wetherell, M. (1987) *Rediscovering the Social Group: A Self-Categorization Theory,* Oxford, Basil Blackwell.

Turner, P.J. (1995) *Sex, Gender and Identity,* Leicester, The British Psychological Society.

FURTHER READING

Sandra Lipsitz Bem (1993) *The Lenses of Gender: Transforming the Debate on Sexual Inequality,* London, Yale University Press. This book argues that, to achieve true gender equality, we need to study the hidden assumptions about sex and gender that pervade our society and culture. Bem's thought-provoking book tries to reveal and then dismantle these assumptions, arguing that society need not – and should not – be organized around the difference between men and women.

Vivien Burr (1998) *Gender and Social Psychology,* London, Routledge. This book gives a clear introduction to the psychology of gender, without assuming a detailed knowledge of psychology. Burr looks at gender differences in a variety of arenas – education, work, and the media – and at some methods used to study gender.

Identity, inequality and social class

Maureen Mackintosh and Gerry Mooney

Contents

1 INTRODUCTION: WORK, INCOMES AND IDENTITY

In Chapter 1, Kath Woodward pointed out how often we ask, 'What is it that you do?' when we meet someone for the first time. This question is not only a means of establishing contact, it also mirrors understandings about how we see ourselves and our world, and how we see others. It presumes a relationship between a person's occupation and his or her identity.

It tends to be paid work that is emphasized in these conversations. Housework or unpaid caring for relatives and family members seem only to define us – as 'carers' or 'housewives' – when we do not also do paid work. This is partly because paid work brings us money to live on. Paid work is also a source of collective identity through relationships with colleagues at work.

In this chapter we examine how income and paid work are closely related sources of individual and collective identity. The pattern of employment and the distribution of incomes are both important structures that shape our identity, as is the way we spend our incomes (our lifestyle). However, there is no simple causal link between what we have and do, and who we are. This is not only because there are other sources of identity besides work and income (as Chapters 1 and 2 showed), it is also because the link between these economic structures and identity is mediated by *representation* (a concept introduced in Chapter 1). How we feel about our job (or lack of one) and our income depends on what others have and how others see us.

Such representations include, for example, classifying some people as 'poor', others as 'working class', yet others as 'middle class'. People may adopt these representations of themselves or they may contest them. One important way in which occupation is linked to identity is thus through the deeply contested notion of social class. The UK is often seen as a class-ridden society. In Chapter 1 for example, an ex-coalminer described the devastation that the wave of closures of mines and heavy industries in the 1980s brought to the identities of people in one working community. In the wake of these kinds of occupational changes, the government announced in 1998 a new social classification of the population, rewritten in terms of newly dominant job categories such as service jobs. Figure 3.1 shows the new classifications and some of the occupations associated with them.

The papers were quick to headline the new social classification 'We're all middle class now'.

The chapter looks at how identities are represented and shaped within economic structures. Section 2 shows how poverty is represented and how being poor shapes identities. Sections 3 and 4 examine some economic structures and focus on inequality, wealth, power and class. Section 5

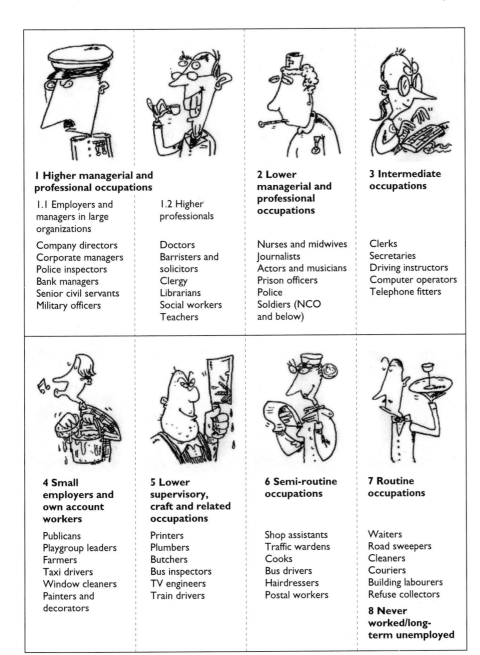

1 Higher managerial and professional occupations

1.1 Employers and managers in large organizations

Company directors
Corporate managers
Police inspectors
Bank managers
Senior civil servants
Military officers

1.2 Higher professionals

Doctors
Barristers and solicitors
Clergy
Librarians
Social workers
Teachers

2 Lower managerial and professional occupations

Nurses and midwives
Journalists
Actors and musicians
Prison officers
Police
Soldiers (NCO and below)

3 Intermediate occupations

Clerks
Secretaries
Driving instructors
Computer operators
Telephone fitters

4 Small employers and own account workers

Publicans
Playgroup leaders
Farmers
Taxi drivers
Window cleaners
Painters and decorators

5 Lower supervisory, craft and related occupations

Printers
Plumbers
Butchers
Bus inspectors
TV engineers
Train drivers

6 Semi-routine occupations

Shop assistants
Traffic wardens
Cooks
Bus drivers
Hairdressers
Postal workers

7 Routine occupations

Waiters
Road sweepers
Cleaners
Couriers
Building labourers
Refuse collectors

8 Never worked/long-term unemployed

FIGURE 3.1 Where you rate in the new social order
Source: *The Guardian*, 15 January 1999, p.3

explores some explanations of social class and Section 6 shifts the emphasis onto consumption as a source of identity. Section 7 revisits the different interpretations of inequality and explores change and uncertainty in the contemporary UK, in the context of social exclusion.

2   WHAT IT IS TO BE POOR

- -

When you say that someone is 'poor', what do you mean?

Do people whom others call 'poor' always see themselves in that way?

One group whose identities are greatly constrained by income are the poor. But, as the questions above suggest, poverty is not a simple fact of some lives: rather, it is a concept with different meanings, and a label that we may accept or reject. This section considers how poverty shapes identity.

2.1   'Making ends meet'

When people talk about being poor, they often talk about the difficulty of being able to 'make ends meet' on low incomes. The phrase evokes people's experience of the daily struggle to feed and clothe a family on very little money, to keep them warm, dry, clean and safe, and to do this without getting into debt or getting into trouble. Some low income families in the UK live on social security benefits alone and have very little other access to cash or formal sources of credit. The result is a very basic existence:

> I don't smoke, I don't drink, I don't go out, I don't eat meat. I have thought of getting rid of the TV but I can't because it's for [my son] ... I think, 'Shall I get rid of the cat?' but I can't ... There's absolutely nothing I spend money on except just surviving, you know, paying bills and buying food.
>
> (quoted in Kempson, 1996, p.49)

This quotation is drawn from a survey of life on low incomes in the early to mid 1990s (Kempson, 1996). The survey was based on 31 studies that had been funded by the Joseph Rowntree Foundation. The people interviewed in the studies were diverse in terms of age, ethnicity, geographical location and life experience. Kempson's survey concluded that people who had been 'on benefits' for a while generally faced a hard choice between going without essentials or falling behind with their bills for water, electricity, gas or rent. The longer people live on low incomes, the harder it gets to cope. Children grow, clothes wear out, appliances need replacing, school activities cost money, isolation gets worse because of lack of money to socialize, and health and mental energy are undermined. Kempson concluded that UK benefit rates in the early 1990s generally gave people insufficient money to cover even basic needs. As one benefit recipient said: 'You're on the poverty line whichever way you look at it ... Nobody can manage on £46 a week. You can't exist on that. You can't manage it. It's degrading' (quoted in Kempson, 1996, p.6).

Many low income households in the UK, however, do not claim state benefits. Many people live on low wages, and the extent of very low paid work increased in the 1980s and 1990s. In the Rowntree studies reported in Kempson, wages of £70–£90 a week for such full time jobs as shop assistant, and around £100 for male manual jobs, were quite commonly reported.

So how much is enough to 'make ends meet'? The Rowntree studies asked this question in a variety of ways. The people interviewed were asked how much money they needed to cover basic outgoings, to live on, to avoid the need to supplement low wages, to create a low likelihood of problem debt. The different calculations produced some remarkably similar answers despite the diversity of people interviewed. Single people reckoned that in the early 1990s they needed about £150 a week, or less if they were not a householder. Lone parents came up with a figure of around £180 a week. Couples with children needed around £200 to avoid arrears on bills. Many people on low wages were working long hours to try to bring their incomes up to these figures (Kempson, 1996).

The consistency of these estimates suggests that, in a particular time and place, there tends to be a shared view about what goods and services are necessities. The UK government also takes a view on this issue. It states that the level of Income Support – the basic benefit for adults – should be 'the amount needed to bring their income up to their "applicable amount". This is the level the law says they need to live on' (DSS, 1997, p.21). Income Support payments vary according to family circumstances and housing costs. The number of people living at or below the Income Support 'poverty line' is frequently used as one definition of those counted as 'poor' in the UK. The Rowntree studies showed that by the early 1990s these benefit payments had fallen below a social consensus on the level that was necessary.

FIGURE 3.2 Urban poverty – Possil Park, Glasgow. In 1998, Possil Park was named the most deprived area in Scotland

2.2 Necessities and luxuries

As the division of opinion between the government and low income people illustrates, definitions of poverty are the stuff of political debate. People in the Rowntree studies tended to focus on 'paying bills and food'. Most people's list of basic needs would also include adequate food and clean water, clothing, shelter and heating. But are there also less apparently physiological, more evidently social, necessities of life?

ACTIVITY 3.1

Look back at the quotation early in this section. A woman on a low income seems to be arguing that a TV is a 'necessity' for her son.

What do you think of her argument? Do you think a TV a 'luxury' or a 'necessity' in the contemporary UK?

Decide what you think and why before reading on.

COMMENT

Televisions were not a necessity in the 1930s since they were not available. But how about in the UK today? You may have answered, no, a TV cannot be a 'necessity' because one can stay alive without a TV. But what about living a human life, with enough sociability and communication to make life worthwhile? Many accounts of the experience of poverty include the pain of social isolation: of not being able to afford to socialize with your peers. Communication with others is part of being human, and in a society where virtually everyone has access to a TV at home, people without television are deprived of access to one of the staples of conversation, jokes and information exchange. Children can suffer particularly from limited access to a shared culture – something the mother quoted above was trying to avoid for her son.

So one might conclude that in the UK, where 96 per cent of households had a television in 1994, it is now a 'necessity'. A lack of a TV constitutes relative deprivation if all the other children in the class have access to one *and* it has become a basic means of communication and cultural reference point. By the same token we could argue that a radio was a necessity in Britain in the 1940s. A TV seems to be a necessity at the end of the twentieth century; a computer may become a necessity in future years if using one becomes a common way to bank, shop and communicate.

There is no 'right answer' to Activity 3.1. Necessities are a matter of social and political judgement. But that does not mean our definitions are arbitrary. In 1990 a study called *Breadline Britain* asked 1800 people whether a number of items were 'necessities'; 58 per cent put a TV in that category, up from 51 per cent in a similar survey in 1983 (Goodman *et al.*, 1997, p.244). Our ideas about what we need depend on what others have and what others expect. Even notions of what constitutes adequate food and heating have changed over time. Social scientists therefore generally recognize that there is a strong 'relative' element in definitions of **poverty**. That is, there are some irreducible human needs, but poverty in a society is also defined relative to the goods, services and opportunities available to the non-poor.

Poverty
Poverty is more than a lack of money. It carries a stigma because it is defined relative to what people think is needed for a decent life.

2.3 How others see us

The relative nature of poverty is an old theme in social science. Adam Smith, the eighteenth century writer who is often regarded as the founding father of economics, put it this way: 'By necessaries I understand not only the commodities that are indispensably necessary for the support of life, but whatever the custom of the country renders it indecent for creditable people, even the lowest orders, to be without' (Smith, 1776, quoted in Sen, 1981).

Ideas of what it is to be poor are thus closely tied up with difficulty in maintaining the basic decencies of life. In the Rowntree studies, people on low incomes repeatedly referred to fear, for example fear of homelessness or disconnection from water, heat and power; to shame, especially shame at getting into debt; and to guilt about having to ask others for help. 'When they turned the water tap off, I felt very upset, I can't explain ... I feel personally ashamed. I feel ashamed at myself' (quoted in Kempson, 1996, p.37).

As a result, the idea of being 'poor' carries a **stigma**: it is a label that many people living on low incomes resist. For example, in a set of interviews in the early 1990s, 85 social security claimants were asked whether they thought 'poverty' existed in Britain, and if so, who were the poor and were they themselves 'poor'? Almost everyone could answer these questions, and almost two thirds of interviewees said that they did not consider themselves to be poor. Half of the rest admitted reluctance in defining themselves as poor. The answers were also gendered. Men were more likely than women to deny poverty, suggesting that men may be more likely to be ashamed and women more realistic, as this short extract from an interview shows:

Stigma
An attribute that is perceived by others as demeaning or discrediting for those who have it. It can be social or physical or a characteristic shared by a whole group or by a few individuals. Stigma is used to justify exclusion.

Interviewer Do you think poverty still exists in this country?

Respondent (man) It don't.

Respondent's wife It does!

Respondent We're not poverty-stricken, nowhere near it yet. We've got all the stuff we can sell.

Respondent's wife But that doesn't mean we've got food in the cupboard ...

(quoted in Dean, 1992, p.83)

The interviewees in the survey expressed many different meanings of the word poverty. Some saw poverty more as a state of mind than a fact: poor people were 'people who think they're poor', an idea often associated with the notion that people bring poverty upon themselves. The survey author comments that some interviewees seemed to see the admission of poverty as a kind of self-indulgence: they insisted that there were many worse off than themselves, or that 'real' poverty no longer existed. Others felt that poverty implied a lack of dignity or cleanliness and cited their clean homes as evidence that they were not poor. Others straightforwardly resisted what they saw as an undesirable classification: some said that they did not 'class' themselves as 'poor', but as 'ordinary working class'.

Poverty is therefore not only a relative matter. Representations of the poor in British culture are often demeaning. As a result of these derogatory meanings, it is hard for people struggling on low incomes to identify themselves as 'poor' and to use that identity in campaigning at the level of national policy. National anti-poverty lobbying has been largely conducted by 'experts' and professional campaign groups. This is in contrast to the effective organization and national lobbying carried out on their own behalf by, for example, people with disabilities (many of whom suffer from poverty) who have fought to change public representations of disability and to change social and individual expectations (Beresford and Croft, 1995). Campaigns of this kind require people to identify with a label; but, as a participant in one conference that brought together anti-poverty campaigners and people with experience of poverty put it: 'I think this word poverty is a real crusher' (Lister and Beresford, 1991, p.10).

FIGURE 3.3
A homeless man begging from commuters

SUMMARY

- Claims about who is *poor* are rooted in shared and contested ideas about the basic necessities of life.

- The experience of *poverty* is both *relative* and *relational*. It is defined by what people have, and what they can do, relative to the opportunities of others.

- *Poverty* carries derogatory meanings, so it does not easily provide a basis for collective identity.

3   WORK, INCOMES AND INEQUALITY

It is not only poverty that is relative and relational: throughout the income scale people define and experience their economic position through ideas about the incomes and opportunities of others. Our identities are, therefore, influenced by the shape of the income distribution. What we mean by this phrase is that it matters to our sense of ourselves whether we imagine that most people's incomes are 'in the middle' or whether we see incomes as polarized between rich and poor. This section takes a look at what the data show.

3.1   Describing inequality

One of the most graphic ways of describing the distribution of incomes is by using the 'income parade' that was invented by a Dutch economist, Jan Pen. It conjures up, in the words of two British economists who have lined up a new UK parade, 'a surreal world where the height of each person in the UK had been stretched in proportion to his or her income, and then everyone was lined up in order of height, the shortest (poorest) on the left and the tallest (richest) on the right' (Jenkins and Cowell, 1994).

Pen imagined his parade passing by in one hour, and talked the reader through the experience. The same can be done using UK data on incomes for the early 1990s, with 56 million people in the line-up. People zip along in the parade with the other members of their household. (All the detail of the UK parade given in this chapter is drawn from Hills, 1995, vol.2.)

The average height in our UK parade is 5ft 8in: that is the height given to each of a couple with average household income. (As the heights given in the Hills report are in feet and inches, we have decided to use these rather than changing them to metric values.) The incomes used in constructing the parade are *household* incomes (otherwise a non-earning partner of an earner would appear – wrongly – as destitute). And the incomes are adjusted – in ways that are described briefly below – for the costs of supporting children and for the numbers of adults in the household. So by 'average' household income we mean the total of these adjusted household incomes divided by the number of households.

So how does the parade look? Bizarre, really. Almost everyone is tiny relative to the few 'giants' who arrive at the end of the parade. After three minutes a single unemployed mother with two small children, living below the Income Support level, goes past: she is about 1ft 10in high. Six minutes later a single male pensioner, owning his own home and claiming Income Support, passes by: he is about 2ft 6in high. Everyone in the first 12 minutes has less than half average incomes, so is below 2ft 10in high. After 21 minutes a childless couple go by: he is a full time vehicle exhaust fitter, she does not do paid work; they are both 3ft 9in high.

You might expect that as the half hour strikes, the people going past will be of average height (that is, average income). But far from being 5ft 8in high, the person who passes you after 30 minutes is only 4ft 10in high, with a household income only 83 per cent of the average. We don't see the household with average income until 62 per cent of the population have passed us. After about 45 minutes, a couple go by with a baby and a toddler: the man is a full time technician in an engineering firm, and the woman works part time as a telephonist. They are both 6ft 10in high.

It is only at ten minutes to the hour that heights really start to grow. With nine minutes to go, a single woman aged 45 without children comes by. She is a full time personnel officer and 8ft 7in high. With three minutes left, a couple in their late fifties whose children have left home pass by. He is a self-employed freelance journalist and she is a part-time manager of a day centre for the elderly. They are both 11ft 11in high. And still the real giants have not arrived. In the last minute a company chief executive and his non-earning wife pass by: they are both at least 60ft high. And in the very last seconds of the parade, the scene changes dramatically. As Pen described those seconds, 'suddenly: the scene is dominated by colossal figures: people like tower flats ... the rear of the parade is brought up by a few participants who are measured in miles ... their heads disappear into the clouds.' (cited in Hills, 1995, vol.2). A modest estimate of the income of Britain's richest man would make him and his partner each four miles high.

This extraordinarily graphic image of income distribution is also very exact. By lining up households in order of income it allows us to compare household incomes, and, as we will now show, to measure changes in inequality over time. Let us look at the parade a little more carefully. Remember, people are classified by household income and that income has been adjusted to allow for the number of people in the household and their ages. The idea is quite simple (though the calculations are not!). Income is based on a couple without children. A single person with an income that is the same as a couple's income will have that income adjusted upwards –

since only one person lives on it, it represents a higher level of income for that one person than for a couple. A couple with children would have the same income adjusted downwards: more people live on it so there is less for each. The resultant 'equivalent' income is what is measured to allocate places in the parade. (Hills, 1995, vol.2; DSS, 1997).

Finally, let's look at those 'averages'. One of the things the income parade shows is that 62 per cent of the UK population lives on less than average income. How can this be? Why is it not 50 per cent? Why *didn't* the 5ft 8in high person zip by on the half hour? The answer lies in the structure of the parade. There are many more poor people than rich, but the top incomes, though very few, are *very* large. So the average (calculated by dividing the total household income by the number of households) is influenced strongly by that couple who are four miles high. The four-mile-highers pull up the average, so the person half-way along the parade has much less than average income.

Suppose we take our UK parade and put in a marker every six minutes. We have then divided our parade into tenths, with the poorest tenth on the left and the richest tenth on the right. We can then pick out the (adjusted) household incomes for the household halfway along each tenth. This gives a picture like that shown in Figure 3.4, which is one representation of the shape of the UK income distribution in the mid 1990s.

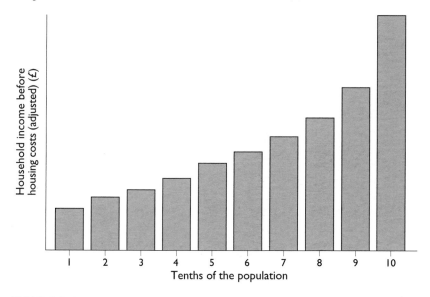

FIGURE 3.4   Tenths of the income distribution, from poor to rich: income of the middle household in each tenth

Source: based on data from DSS, 1997, Table A2

ACTIVITY 3.2

Look carefully at Figure 3.4. Looking along the bottom, you can see that each bar represents a tenth of the population, with the poorest tenth at the left, just as in the income parade. The height of the bar represents the adjusted household income for the household half-way along each tenth. The income is measured up the vertical axis in £s. If you look at Figure 3.4. you will see that there is no scale on the vertical axis, this is because we want you to examine your own perceptions of the UK income distribution.

Think back to the mid 1990s. To get into the *top tenth* of the income distribution, that is, to be better off than 90 per cent of the UK population, how much do you think a single person would have needed to earn? How about a childless couple or a couple with two children? Remember that a single person needs less for the same standard of living than a couple with children. If you get a chance, ask a few other people their opinions.

Try to guess before you look at the answer given at the end of the chapter: this activity is about perceptions of inequality, not a test of general knowledge!

COMMENT

How did you get on? Guesses vary of course, but it is common for people to overestimate what you need to earn to live better than 90 per cent of the population. Politicians make this kind of mistake all the time. They have been known to refer to £30,000 a year as 'middle income', whereas those earnings would take even a couple with children into the top 30 per cent of the income distribution. It is also common to underestimate just how much difference children make, that is, how expensive they really are! The person half-way along the parade described above is one of a childless couple with one person earning a little more than £16,000 a year (Goodman *et al.*, 1997).

This activity also illustrates how socially and economically varied the top tenth is. A single person earning £22,000 has little in common with the merchant bankers and business directors at the very end of the parade. The income differences within the top tenth are *far* larger than elsewhere: that was one point of the parade.

3.2 Increasing inequality

Inequality in incomes got worse during the 1980s and early 1990s. Dividing the income parade into tenths offers us a neat way of displaying this increasing inequality. Look first at Figure 3.5. Each of the vertical bars shows the percentage change in income between 1961 and 1979 for the person who occurs mid-way along each of the tenths of the population, lined up as in our parade. The higher the bar, the higher the percentage change. So the poorest tenth of the population had an increase in income of over 50 per cent. (These are 'real' incomes; that is, adjusted to take out the effects of general price inflation and to estimate what the incomes will buy.) The other tenths had an increase of about one third. So overall, the people at the beginning of the parade got a *little* larger (but only by a very small amount) relative to the people coming by later on (Hills, 1996).

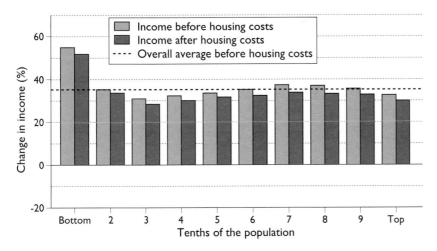

FIGURE 3.5 Change in real after-tax income, by tenths of the population, 1961–79
Source: Hills, 1996, p.4

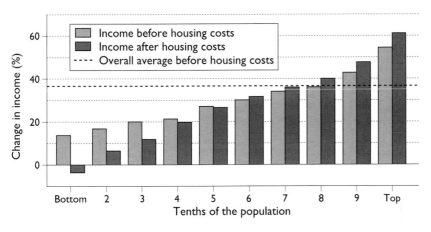

FIGURE 3.6 Change in real after-tax income, by tenths of the population, 1979–1994/5
Source: DSS, 1997, p.69

Between 1979 and 1994–5, within the years of Conservative government, a quite different pattern emerges. The contrast is genuinely startling. In those years, as Figure 3.6 shows, the increases in income were concentrated in the better-off tenths of the population. The pattern is consistent. The richest tenth got the largest percentage increase, then the next, and so on down to the poorest. Furthermore, if the incomes are calculated after people have paid for housing – an essential expenditure with costs that vary hugely across the country – then those people earliest in the parade actually shrank: the poorest tenth of the population saw their income fall. Income distribution in the years shown in Figure 3.6 became much more unequal (DSS, 1997; Hills, 1996).

So in the 1980s and early 1990s the gap between poor and rich widened dramatically. There was a significant rise in the numbers in poverty, as measured by income. A common measure of numbers in poverty is those who are living in households at or below half of average (adjusted) incomes. In our early 1990s parade, everyone in the first two tenths fell into this group. Between 1979 and 1991–2 the number of people living in households at or below half of average incomes (after housing costs) rose from 5.0 million to 13.9 million. Of those 13.9 million, 6.0 million had incomes below half the *1979* average (Hills, 1995, p.32).

Given the number of people involved, 'the poor' are, of course, very diverse. If you are a single parent (most of whom are female) or unemployed then you are very likely to find yourself in this group. A third of single pensioners and 27 per cent of households supported by part time workers are there too. The risk of poverty is high for the long-term sick and for people with disabilities. Members of some ethnic minorities are also much more likely than the white population to find themselves in the bottom fifth of the income distribution (Goodman *et al.*, 1997). This diversity shows how being 'poor' interacts with other sources of identity, such as gender and ethnicity.

SUMMARY

- The UK income distribution is highly unequal, and has been becoming more so.
- Well over half the UK population live below average incomes.
- A few wealthy people have extraordinarily high incomes relative to everyone else.
- The numbers in poverty rose sharply in the 1980s and early 1990s.
- Important determinants of where you are in the income distribution are occupation and household structure, including the number of children within the household.

4 WEALTH, POWER AND CLASS

The further you are down the income distribution, the more you are likely to experience income as a structural constraint. The wealthier you are, conversely, the more you may be aware of income and wealth as sources of opportunity and of power over others.

4.1 Wealth and class identity

Income is very unequal in the UK, but wealth holding is even more dramatically unequal. Data on the very wealthy are hard to collect, but according to the Inland Revenue (the only collectors of non-voluntary data!) in 1994 over half (53 per cent) the **financial wealth** in the UK was owned by 5 per cent of the population (ONS, 1998, p.104). Conversely, most people have virtually no financial cushion. The less wealthy half of the UK population has less than £500 per household in savings (and owns only 6 per cent in total of the financial wealth), while the least wealthy quarter has savings of less than £50 (Banks *et al.*, 1996; Hills, 1995; ONS, 1998).

Financial wealth
This includes savings, company shares, interest-earning loans and insurance policies.

Wealth and privilege are not very visible. The wealthy can withdraw into a private world of fee-paying schooling, private transport and health care, and social networks that are largely invisible to the non-wealthy. People in Britain, when asked to identify the privileged, tend to refer to an aristocracy or landed

FIGURE 3.7 Wealthy picnickers at Henley Royal Regatta: such images figure prominently in representations of the UK's 'upper class'

class, rather than their own managers and employers (Scott, 1994). This 'them and us', 'rich and poor' notion of social class is weakening but it is still influential and is fed by media images of the 'upper class' whose relationships and activities are represented in the popular media as being of enormous interest.

The weakening of these particular class distinctions is, in part, due to the spreading of private non-financial wealth downwards in the UK in the last 50 years. Houses and pension funds are also a form of wealth: 66 per cent of homes are now privately owned; 75 per cent of men working full time and 65 per cent of women working full time have occupational or individual private pensions. This is not 'wealth' in quite the same sense as financial assets: since we need them to live in and on, we cannot sell our houses and pensions without replacing them in some form. However, these forms of private wealth underpin 'middle class' living standards and self-perceptions. Adding them to financial wealth makes wealth distribution less unequal but even so the less wealthy half of the population still only own 10 per cent of the UK's wealth between them.

4.2 Wealth, capital and power

Wealth – even very modest wealth – brings some security and control. But among the wealthy, financial wealth and power are associated in a different way: wealth confers power over the lives of others. The very rich in the UK are either landowners, with inherited fortunes in landed property (particularly in urban areas), or they own fortunes derived from – and held in part as – shares in – manufacturing and service industries. Some of the richest landowners are from the old peerage: for example the Duke of Westminster's family estate includes much of Mayfair and Belgravia. Those holding fortunes in industry, commerce and finance are more diverse in origin. They include the inheritors of family industrial fortunes, such as the Sainsbury and the Pearson families. They also include first generation entrepreneurial wealth. The music business and computing have been routes for such self-made fortunes including, for example, those made by Alan Sugar who built up Amstrad, and Richard Branson of Virgin who started from a well-off professional background and made his first million selling hit records (Brown, 1988; Scott, 1994).

Most of the very wealthy are employers, either indirectly, through owning large shareholdings in companies, or as company directors. While the rest of us – if we own anything – usually have wealth in the form of houses and pensions, the top 1 per cent (those with wealth over £500,000 in 1994) held around 40 per cent of their wealth in company shares (Hills, 1995, p.98). A group of those with high incomes and wealth also work at managing the financial assets of others. Consider pension funds for example. You may have an occupational or private pension. If you do, the money you put into it each year will be managed on your behalf – and generally without your participation – by pension fund managers. They invest the funds: they lend them to governments and large companies, they buy commercial property to rent out and they buy company shares. Economists call finance used in this way 'capital'. It operates as the key link between wealth and power.

Wealthy business people thus invest their own capital and – predominantly – the capital of others in equipping businesses, in employing people and in producing goods and services. They respond to market opportunities in ways that shape our working lives. This economic system – the one within which most people in the world now live – is called **capitalism**.

Although historically relatively recent (barely two centuries old), capitalism has driven vast economic and social transformations. There has been a huge rise in total output of goods and services and enormous changes in the way we work and live, including huge international as well as national divergences in living standards. The perceived division capitalism has generated between those who own and manage capital and those who are employed is another enduring element of our notions of social class.

Capitalism
A system driven by the investment of private capital in large-scale production activities in pursuit of private profit.

SUMMARY

- Financial wealth is concentrated in few hands.
- Housing and pension wealth is somewhat more dispersed.
- Management of financial wealth as capital confers power.
- Both wealth, and power as an employer, are sources of class distinction.

5 SOCIAL CLASS

5.1 Seeing ourselves in class terms

Section 4 introduced two key elements of popular notions of social class: class as hierarchy, where those at the top do best, and class as oppositional, between those who own capital and those they employ. The *British Social Attitudes Survey* provides one regular source of evidence of how class permeates people's understanding of society. The 1995–96 edition showed that 69 per cent of people surveyed thought that a person's social class affected his or her opportunities a 'great deal' or 'quite a lot' (Jowell *et al.*, 1995). In a different 1996 survey, two-thirds of those interviewed agreed that 'there is one law for the rich and one for the poor' and that 'ordinary people do not get their fair share of the nation's wealth' (Adonis and Pollard, 1998, p.11).

Social class can provide us with a sense of belonging; it can tell us who 'we' are and who 'they' are and, hence, how to relate to the world around us. Many people see the UK as a society sharply divided by class divisions and inequalities, but it does not follow that individuals have a strongly developed sense of class identity. Whether, or how strongly, you identify yourself as a member of a social class will be shaped by your personal history, including your family background, your occupation and your personal experiences of struggle and conflict. While some people, such as the interviewee quoted in Section 2, see 'working class' as a positive label they can identify with, others reject the term as stigmatizing or patronizing.

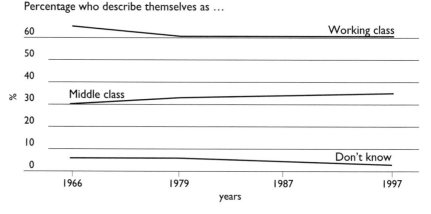

FIGURE 3.8   Most people in Britain still describe themselves in class terms, and a majority still see themselves as working class
Source: *The Guardian*, 15 January 1999, p.3

Many sociologists argue that class has lost much of its significance for identity, some go so far as suggesting that 'class is dead' (Pakulski and Waters, 1996). The evidence offered for these claims mixes changing social and economic structures and the rise of other sources of identity and belonging. In the immediate post-war era, large-scale manufacturing and mining employed far more people than in the 1990s, and working-class identification was reflected in mass membership of organizations such as the Labour Party, trade unions, and work-based social and political clubs. Many of these organized sources of identity were dominated by, or exclusive to, men. The rise of mass unemployment in the 1970s and 1980s, the shift to service industries and the increase in the number of women working led to many of these institutions fragmenting, and membership dropped. An identification with work-based community cultures may have declined with it.

Other work-based structural changes reinforced this erosion of identities based on work. As national collective bargaining declined, trade unionism fragmented into more sectional identities. The Labour Party leadership worked hard in the 1990s to shed any identification of the party with the working class, seeking the 'middle' social ground. Work-based identities have also been cross-cut with other sources of identity. The rising importance of gender and ethnic identities and the emphasis in the mass media on diverse consumption-based lifestyles, has reinforced awareness that individuals play an active role in the construction of their own identity.

Social class is both a central and a highly contested concept within social science: there is little agreement over its meaning, measurement, or how it should be used as an explanatory device. However, as a field of social scientific inquiry, social class is dominated by two distinctive traditions of thought – Marxism and Weberianism. These traditions are rooted in the writings of Karl Marx (1818–1883) and Max Weber (1864–1920). While Marx and Weber differ in important ways in their understanding of class and society, both share a view of classes as groups structured out of economic relationships. Upon this central foundation, successive generations of social scientists have reworked and reformulated the arguments of Marx and Weber in the light of social, economic and political change. Each tradition brings together, in distinctive ways, an analysis of the economic roots of class, and a perspective on representation and the construction of class identities. The rest of this section explores some central ideas of these two living traditions within the social sciences.

5.2 The Marxist theory of class

Marx and his close associate Friedrich Engels were responsible for a theory of class that has been important both for its intellectual influence upon subsequent generations of social scientists, and for its wider political influence. Marx's ideas were a product of nineteenth century European and British society. When Marx was writing, European society was going through a period of profound upheaval and transformation. The Industrial Revolution had brought new industries and occupations to the ever-expanding towns and cities, where much of the working class population lived in dreadful conditions. This was also a period of profound political change, as newly emerging social groups struggled for power. Trade unions were developing, and the new industrial working classes increasingly fought for better working conditions, better housing and education, and political representation. Marx's theory of class reflects this period of social upheaval and conflict.

Marx's theory of **class** was part of a much wider project of explaining the historical emergence of industrial capitalism, as this new type of society was called, and its main driving forces. He saw the key defining feature of a society as being the way in which goods and wealth are produced. The organization and ownership of the means of production – tools, machines, workplaces and raw materials – shape the social relationships between individuals and groups within a society. The factories being constructed in mid-nineteenth century Britain were the means of production of the industrial capitalist system. The owners of capital, that is, of the financial wealth invested in the new manufacturing processes, were identified by Marx as the new ruling class.

Marx and class
For Marxists, class is rooted in the economic organization of production.

For Marx and Engels, capitalist society generated two main classes, or as they put it , 'two great warring and hostile camps' (Marx and Engels, 1848, p.49), a capital-owning class and a propertyless class, who occupied different positions in the organization of production. They called these classes the 'bourgeoisie' and the 'proletariat', or the ruling class and the working class. In return for their labours, the workers received a wage but the products of their labour were appropriated by capitalists and sold for profit, a process that Marx called *exploitation*.

There is much more that could be said about Marx's analysis of class but here we want to emphasize just three themes that have considerable continuing force in the way we think about class identities. First is the link between individual economic position within systems of production – specifically the ownership of capital – and class position. For Marx and later Marxists, class is a structure rooted in the economic organization of production.

Second is the idea of social polarization and associated class conflict. Marx expected that as capitalism developed, big business would gradually squeeze out all the small-scale capitalists, the self-employed and the small shop-owners. The result would be a growing divide between the bourgeoisie and a proletariat who were constantly threatened with impoverishment. Later industrial capitalism – at least in the more developed countries – has created a better-off and more differentiated workforce than this vision imagined. But scope for new forms of social polarization remains (see Section 7).

Class consciousness
An awareness of a shared class interest and of the existence of classes with opposing interests.

Third, Marx's emphasis on **class consciousness** is particularly relevant to our understanding of identity. Marx stressed class conflict in all his writings, but he did not see class conflict as inevitable. According to Marx, two factors were necessary for a fully developed proletarian class to exist: *objective* factors, that is, workers who share the same relationship to the means of production, and *subjective* factors. The latter refer to an awareness of a shared class position and of the existence of other classes with opposing class interests. This is how Marx describes the birth of the working class and its consciousness:

> Economic conditions had first transformed the mass of the people of the country into workers. The domination of capital has created for this mass a common situation, common interests. The mass is thus already a class against capital, but not yet for itself. In the struggle ... this mass becomes united, and constitutes itself as a class for itself. The interests it defends become class interests.
>
> (Marx and Engels, 1983, p.211)

Thus full class consciousness only emerges though the experience of solidarity and collective action. Marx put forward a strong notion of collective class identity which was rooted in economic structures that he saw as inherently conflictual, and developed through collective action in the experience of organization and class struggle.

Marxism, then, sees social relationships and human action as being constrained by the economic structures of society, but argues that those structures also generate the conditions for collective consciousness and identity. The development of a new type of society necessitates collective, not individual, action.

FIGURE 3.9 *Solidarity and collective action: Members of the Greater London Pensioners Organization contrasting levels of city pay to the level of their pensions, January 1998*

FIGURE 3.10 *Solidarity and collective action: Tameside Care Group workers waving to supporters while demonstrating against*

5.3 Max Weber's theory of social stratification

Max Weber, one of the founders of the discipline of sociology, was writing at the time of the major social upheavals that gripped European societies just before and after the First World War. Weber's perspective, and the tradition of social analysis based upon it, offers an alternative vision of social class to that put forward by Marx.

Weber is credited with drawing attention to forms of *stratification* other than class, in particular to divisions of status and what he calls 'party'. 'Party', in Weber's writings, refers to any organization or voluntary association that brings together people with common backgrounds, aims or interests in pursuit of particular policies or control of a particular organization. (The relationship between 'party' and political power is explored more fully in **Hughes and Fergusson, 2000, Chapter 4**.) Like Marx, Weber recognizes the existence of economically defined social classes, but his starting point is individuals. In Weberian sociology, **class** refers to identifiable groups of individuals who have certain interests in common. These common interests can be summarized as market position, that is, individuals having similar opportunities for earning income through work or trade.

Weber and class
Weberians see class as being rooted in market position.

Different class groupings thus have distinct market situations which either privilege them or make them more vulnerable. Because of privileged access to the means of production and consumption, members of certain groups will enjoy better 'life chances' than others. Life chances refer to opportunities for education, health, housing, employment and levels of income. The key point is that for Weberians, class divisions and inequalities reflect different life chances in the market, whereas for Marxists, class relationships are founded in exploitative production relations.

Weber, like Marx, identifies a division between propertied and propertyless classes, but he also highlights divisions within those classes, divisions that are the product of differential reward by the market. For example, professional employees tend to find themselves in a privileged position in the market relative to semi-skilled workers. Markets operate in a way that divide and sub-divide classes. As a result, the differentiation between groups of employees becomes increasingly complex.

Status
The prestige, honour or social standing attached to different social groups.

For Weber, this fragmentation of classes is accentuated by differences in **status**, that is, the different amount of prestige, honour or social standing that society attaches to different social groups. Thus status relies on people's subjective evaluation of social differences: '"Classes" are stratified according to their relations to the production and acquisition of goods; whereas "status groups" are stratified according to the principles of their consumption of goods as represented by special "styles of life"' (Weber, quoted in Hughes, 1984, p.8).

Membership of a particular status group may confer certain benefits or rewards, or prohibit people from access to them. For example, members of different ethnic minority or religious groups may find themselves alternatively privileged or prohibited in this respect, *irrespective of their class position*. Hence, different groups may find themselves occupying similar economic class positions while being distinguished by differences in status, and status may be more significant than class as a source of identity. Groups may also experience inequalities in power deriving from party, that is, from the ability to organize themselves to further their own interests and to marginalize others. Weber thus sees class, status and party as cross-cutting, with class more concerned with the production of goods and status with their consumption. This vision of social fragmentation and increasing social diversity contrasts sharply with the Marxist image of class-based social polarization.

5.4 Class and identity in the two traditions

ACTIVITY 3.3

This activity asks you to try to apply these two traditions to an example of new types of paid work. Read the case study of call centres in Box 3.1 and then write some notes in answer to the following question.

How would social scientists in the tradition of (a) Marx and (b) Weber analyse the class position of call centre workers?

Try to bring issues of class consciousness and status into your argument.

BOX 3.1   Case study of call centres

Helplines, centralized telephone enquiry handling, direct sales and service, telephone banking, mortgage lending and insurance, teleconferencing: there has been an explosion in the 1990s of large call centres handling all these types of telephone-based activity. Section 4 introduced the concept of capital investment as a major force structuring our working lives; call centres are an example of this. In the 1990s, new firms mushroomed to undertake direct selling and customer services, and existing firms invested large sums in centralizing or creating these activities, in order to reduce costs or fight off competition from new, wholly telephone-based companies such as *First Direct*.

A call centre is basically a large room where people sit at banks of telephones making and answering calls. By 1997 call centres employed about 300,000 people; this is expected to grow to half a million – more than 2 per cent of the workforce – by the year 2000 (*Financial Times*, 29 November 1998). The jobs are concentrated in particular areas, including central Scotland, Tyneside and the

FIGURE 3.11   Answering calls at *First Direct*, Leeds

West Country, where unemployment is high and labour is thought to be relatively cheap. A survey in Scotland in 1997 found 108 call centres, a third with over 500 employees, and plans for new large centres employing thousands (Taylor and Bain, 1999). Glasgow Development Agency is actively campaigning for call centre investment in the city.

Call centre employment, however, has a problematic reputation (Fernie and Metcalfe, 1997; *The Guardian*, 2 June 1998). Call centres have been called the 'new sweatshops' and 'white collar factories'. Call centre jobs are distinctive in the integration of telephone and computer technology: the 'agents' or 'representatives' answer queries and sell goods and services on the telephone while looking up and entering information on computer screens. New technology increases work rates: 'Dialling manually you can only make thirty calls and maybe speak to 10 people. The power dialler will get 80 phone calls and you'll speak to every one of them in a 4-hour shift' (quoted in Taylor and Bain, 1999).

Staff can see a display of the waiting calls stacked up for them, and they know that the time they take on calls and the money they bring in when selling are automatically monitored. The result is an 'assembly line in the head' (Taylor and Bain, 1999).

There are other forms of stress too. Staff have to work not only fast but pleasantly. They need to be 'natural' and to 'smile down the phone' – even when customers are rude or confusing. They need to follow a script, repetitively, while making each encounter seem personal to the caller. Staff are monitored not only by machine but also by supervisors listening in to their tone and manner. Some firms try to encourage 'teams' of employees to compete with each other. Some monitor, and even restrict, toilet visits.

The call centre workforce is predominantly young and female, and centres frequently organize shifts to fit round domestic activities. Wages are generally higher than, for example, shop counter jobs, but mental fatigue, voice-loss and depression are quite common, and turnover can be high – 30 per cent per year in some firms. Staff are generally set targets, for example for sales value per team per week (Taylor, 1998) and performance-related pay is quite common. Targets for speed and sales are often raised to increase pressure on staff.

One indicator of employees' resistance to some aspects of call centre work is unionization. Increasing numbers of call centres, especially the large ones, are unionized. Half of the Scottish centres in the 1997 survey had a union or a staff association. Unions trying to recruit, such as BIFU, CWU and Unison, have concentrated on work conditions (in one centre, it took unionization to get staff a tea break), health and safety at work, pay and holidays, rights for part-time staff (projected to be half the call centre workforce in Scotland by 2000), and limitations on uncontrolled monitoring of employees by supervisors.

COMMENT

There are a number of points you might have made in answer to the question. Here are just a few.

In the Marxist tradition, call centre employment would be analysed in terms of the relationship between the employer and the employee. In order to increase rates of work, new technology brings the pressures of the production line into 'white collar' work. A Marxist would see call centre workers as working class and point to rising discontent, resistance and unionization as evidence of growing class consciousness and a sense of collective work-place identity.

A Weberian would also identify elements of class: a group of individuals sharing a similar position in the labour force. Weberians would, however, highlight the use of mostly young female workers, stressing gender as a dimension of inequality of status affecting market position but not reducible to class. They might point to the emphasis on individual skill, internal competition between workers, and performance-related pay as fragmenting the workforce, and might see unionization as the pursuit of sectional interests rather than evidence of collective identity.

SUMMARY

- Both traditions see class and class divisions as rooted in economic structures.
- In Marxism, class is structured by the ownership and organization of production; in Weberianism, class is structured by market position.
- Class is more central to the Marxist tradition than to the Weberian tradition.
- Weberians identify non-class elements of social stratification, notably status and party, that are independent of social class.
- Class consciousness – involving identification as a member of a class – in the Marxist tradition emerges through collective action.
- Identity and collective action in the Weberian tradition focus more on status group than on class.

6 AN EROSION OF CLASS IDENTITY?

Section 5 began by considering some of the claims made about the extent of class divisions in the UK today. As we saw, a popular argument in both the social sciences and political debate is that the 'old' certainties of social class have been eroded. In the late 1990s, the issue of class was given renewed prominence by the Labour Prime Minister's claim that:

> Slowly but surely, the old establishment is being replaced by a new, larger, more meritocratic middle class.
>
> A middle class characterised by greater tolerance of difference, greater ambition to succeed, greater opportunities to earn a decent living.
>
> A middle class that will include millions of people who traditionally may see themselves as working class, but whose ambitions are far broader than those of their parents and grandparents.
>
> (Tony Blair, quoted in *The Guardian*, 15 January 1999, p.3)

Similar arguments have been made by sociologists and political scientists, not only in the 1980s and 1990s, but also in the 1950s and 1960s. Two claims recur: there has been a move from collective to individual identities and also there has been a move from occupation to consumption patterns as sources of social distinction.

In the early 1960s, with the experience of a booming economy and rising consumption plus three general election victories for the Conservatives in 1951, 1955 and 1959, it was widely argued that well-paid sections of the working class were increasingly adopting middle-class values and lifestyles, thus eroding working-class identities. A study of attitudes and class identity among car workers at Vauxhall's Luton car plant (Goldthorpe *et al.*, 1969) concluded that there was little evidence to support these claims, but there were signs that working-class identity was fragmenting and a growing differentiation among a 'new' working class was developing.

The researchers argued that the new working class were distinguished by 'instrumentalism', that is, simply working for money. Work played a smaller role in their sense of identity than it did for the 'traditional' working class, with 'non-work' life, that is, family and home, playing a more important role. A sense of class identity, characteristic of the traditional working class, was being eroded by a more home-centred or 'privatized' and individualistic sense of identity. (That the Luton car workers went on strike only weeks after the study was completed failed to dispel claims that a 'new' working class was in the making.)

6.1 Class and consumption

The idea that class, as a structural factor shaping outlook on life and sense of social identity, was being replaced by non-work-based sources of identity reappeared vigorously in the 1980s and 1990s, once more in a context of widespread social and economic change and successive election victories for the Conservatives. Peter Saunders, an influential British sociologist, argued in the 1980s that consumption processes and differences in lifestyle had become more important than occupation-based class in constructing identities and in explaining social behaviours and attitudes (Saunders, 1984). In particular, he and others argued that the decline in votes for the Labour Party was largely due to the emergence of new consumption cleavages.

Voting preferences have long been identified by political scientists and sociologists as one of the key indicators for assessing the prevalence of *class identification*. The period following 1945 is said to be characterized by **class alignment**, that is, people tended to vote along class lines, with the working class predominantly voting Labour and the middle and upper classes opting for the Conservatives. Working-class Conservatives were seen as a puzzle requiring explanation. Conversely, Labour's declining share of the vote in the 1980s and early 1990s was attributed to class dealignment, reflecting an erosion of class and work-based sources of identity.

Class alignment
People tending to vote along class lines.

Saunders argued that a major process of 'social restratification' was taking place during this period, with a growing division between a 'middle mass' of those who could increasingly satisfy their consumption needs through private ownership of cars, housing and even private education and health care, and those who remained insecurely dependent on state provision of housing, public transport, education and health care. He predicted: 'an increasingly visible fault line in British society, not along the lines of class, but on the basis of private ownership of the means of consumption' (Saunders, 1984, p.211).

Saunders was not only arguing that new forms of stratification have emerged, but also that these are independent of work and class-based social divisions. Thus divisions of consumption and lifestyle cut across 'old' class lines, with consumption now influencing and shaping identity and social attitudes to a far greater extent.

Saunders' arguments were widely criticized for their failure to show that consumption directly influences people's identities and attitudes, such as political preferences. Critics noted that studies such as Saunders' continued to point to occupational class as a powerful influence on income, consumption and political attitudes and identities (Crompton, 1998).

Both the Luton researchers in the 1960s and Saunders in the 1980s claim that after 1945 UK society became increasingly individualized. The Luton study made this claim in a context of rising economic prosperity. By contrast, in the decades that followed, sociologists attributed individualization to the increasing insecurity of employment that forced individuals to negotiate their own path through unstable labour markets. So both prosperity and insecurity may lead to individualization and a move away from workplace-based identities, as illustrated in the John Greaves example in Chapter 1. In the 1980s, employment instability is argued to have eroded workplace and occupational communities, and forced people to see their working lives as unstable personal journeys. In place of collective work-based identities, individuals constructed their images of themselves much more around consumption and lifestyles.

Pierre Bourdieu, a French sociologist, has examined the interrelationship between class and consumption through empirical studies of consumption habits. In his book *Distinction*, Bourdieu explores the ways in which people express their identity through consumption (Bourdieu, 1984). Because consumption tastes are one way we distinguish ourselves from others, consumption patterns differentiate both *within* and *between* classes. In this way, he argues, consumption both establishes and expresses social difference. People invest effort as well as money in consumption, and two people with similar incomes but different economic class positions will be likely to have very different consumption patterns. Bourdieu, who looks explicitly back to both Marx and Weber, sees occupational class and consumption as interrelated, not opposing, influences on identity.

ACTIVITY 3.4

Make a list of some ways in which consumption patterns and preferences differ between social classes, and consider how far we are able to make choices about consumption patterns.

COMMENT

You might have mentioned differences between working-class and middle-class people in television viewing habits, clothing and food preferences, musical tastes, home decoration, choice of cars and holidays. Note that Bourdieu, like other social scientists, is not arguing that all individuals conform to class-related consumption patterns; he is interested, rather, in the way that cultural practices such as consumption preferences are highly symbolic markers of status and class distinction. As a result, it can be hard for a member of a particular status or occupational group to sustain a consumption pattern very different from that expected of him or her. Finally, as Section 2 made clear, low incomes limit consumption choices very sharply indeed.

SUMMARY

- Class as a source of collective identity may be being eroded by a more individualistic and consumerist culture.

- Some sociologists argue that consumption has replaced class as the key factor structuring social division and identities.

- Sociologists such as Bourdieu also emphasize consumption as a major influence on identity, but analyse consumption as an expression of differentiation within and between classes.

7 SOCIAL POLARIZATION AND SOCIAL EXCLUSION

7.1 A polarizing society?

If you look back at the different understandings of inequality that have run through this chapter from Section 3 onwards, you can perhaps divide them into two camps. There is one set that sees inequality as gradations in a hierarchy. The 'income parade' fits in here: it shows how many more people live below than above average incomes, and how few and wealthy are the rich, but there are no sharp breaks in the parade. You might see Weber's complex mix of class position and status in the same light, and Bourdieu too: inequality in society is complex, and hierarchical, with cross-cutting identities. There are no sharp breaks.

Social exclusion
Some groups are marginalized and excluded from full participation and from taking advantage of all that is available to the more affluent in society.

Social polarization
A growing social divide between a relatively affluent majority and a large excluded minority.

Then there is the other camp: theorists who spot fault lines or cleavages, and emphasize conflict. These views are found right across the political spectrum; they include Marxists and also sociologists like Saunders who emphasize consumption cleavages. This image of a social divide re-entered the middle ground of UK politics in the late 1990s, with the Blair government's emphasis on the problem of **social exclusion**. The government's policies are underpinned by the argument that Britain displays a growing polarization between a relatively affluent majority and a large excluded minority.

Those arguing that there is **social polarization** do have some evidence on their side. In addition to the widening inequality, low wage rates and low benefit levels described in Sections 2 and 3, there has been a profound change in the distribution of work across households (Buck *et al.*, 1994; Gregg and Wadsworth, 1996; Harkness *et al.*, 1998). Since the early 1980s, the proportion of households with a single earner has declined sharply; households with more than one earner have increased in number. And, while in 1979 just 1 in 10 households had no paid earner, by 1994–5 this had increased to 1 in 5 (DSS, 1998, p.41). This emerging division between 'work poor' and 'work rich' households appears to interact with other influences in creating an 'excluded' group whose chances of getting into, or back into, paid employment are very low. Reflecting this, the new Office of National Statistics (ONS) social classification, which was referred to in the introduction to this chapter and illustrated in Figure 3.1, and which will be used in the 2001 census, has a new 'class 8' category for those who have never worked and are unlikely to do so.

Furthermore, while some of the so-called 'work rich' households have two professional earners and are well within the top tenth of the income distribution, many multiple-earner households cope on several low, insecure incomes. Unemployment remains high in the UK, and wages and insecurity of employment at the lower end have worsened. Relatively low-skilled work has become casualized, is predominantly female and displays a high rate of staff turnover (Pinch, 1993). Some of the call centre work discussed in Section 5 comes into this category (and call centres themselves may be superseded by new forms of technology, such as e-commerce, in a few years time). Data on household incomes over time shows that fluctuations and insecurity of incomes are far more prevalent among low income groups than among the better off. The experience of recurrent poverty affects many more than those who are poor at any one time (Gardiner and Hills, 1999).

Finally, the deterioration of public services and infrastructures in the 1980s and 1990s reinforced social polarization. Poverty and unemployment are geographically highly concentrated, notably in parts of the inner cities and on large housing estates. Higher charges and declining standards in public transport, education, housing and the health services have a cumulatively worse impact on those who rely on them most (see **Hughes and Fergusson, 2000**). Saunders' arguments have some leverage here: as the public sector deteriorates, it contributes to trapping those who cannot 'go private' into poverty.

There is some good economic evidence, then, for social polarization. However, the argument becomes much more problematic and contested when it moves from incomes and employment to culture and identity. Some commentators, (such as the influential US commentator Charles Murray) see social polarization as creating a so-called 'underclass'. They argue that such communities generate a distinct culture of resistance, characterized by criminality and avoidance of employment. This argument has been widely criticized as stigmatizing the disadvantaged. So do people have distinct identities, shaped by different attitudes to income and paid work, in 'excluded' communities?

7.2 Uncertainty and identity

At the end of the 1980s, the sociologist Bill Jordan and a group of colleagues set out to answer this question through detailed interviewing of families on one outer-city council estate in southern England. In their study *Trapped in Poverty?*, the researchers argue that the families they studied held ideas about what their roles should be in work and in the family that were no different from those of the rest of society. They did not see themselves as excluded or as members of an 'underclass'. What was different, however, was the difficulty of making sense of their work-related identities when faced with the economic pressures upon them.

The predominant experience of the interviewees was insecurity. A minority of men had regular long-term employment and they were all well aware of its value and its fragility. Almost all the men had been unemployed. All the men talked of needing to work, and idleness was characterized as boring and destructive of identity and self-respect (Jordan *et al.*, 1992, p.99). The men made sense of their lives through narratives about how they managed insecurity and the difficulty of finding work. In explaining how they saw themselves and their working lives, the men drew on familiar categories. They all, without exception, saw the proper role of a man as a breadwinner.

Men without regular work emphasized the importance of networks and knowledge in trying to find work. Some with irregular earnings characterized themselves as 'self employed', drawing on the language of enterprise and self-help – much emphasized by the politicians of the time – as a source of identity and self respect. Some men and women had bought or had discussed buying their homes, but this was as a source of stability and connection, not as a means of disconnection from the estate.

The women coped in similarly familiar terms. They emphasized women's primary responsibility for child care and household work, and drew on networks of female kin and friends to help them combine this with seeking employment. The vast majority of the households relied on women's contributions to total income, and in a minority of households women were the main earners. But even in the latter, women tended to emphasize their household role – even if they admitted to boredom with it – in explaining how they saw their approach to work. Some talked about 'spreading their wings' as the children got older, through employment and education.

The researchers emphasize that people on the estate were applying familiar norms and sources of identity to coping with a very difficult economic context. A good example is the attitude to casual work and unreported earnings. Both men and women were well aware of the problems posed by the benefits system for those trying earn a decent living: earning more or taking work could lead to benefits being withdrawn, so people got stuck in a 'trap' of poverty and unemployment. Everyone saw this as unfair and, as a result, regarded some undeclared cash work as normal and legitimate. But all constructed limits on how much it was 'fair' to earn and criticized (and occasionally informed on) those who drastically over-stepped the mark. The shared sense of fair, undeclared earnings was felt to be around £30-50 a week, well over the legal limit (£5 at the time), but far from extreme (Jordan *et al.*, 1992, p.319).

This resistance to legal rules – and the creation of informal local norms – was in the service of a work ethic and family responsibility, not as a method of avoidance. Note that the interviewers in this study were not seeking one 'true' story about what people do – perspectives differ within households, and some things may be hidden – but rather a sense of how people saw themselves in relation to paid work, how they would explain and justify themselves. The researchers found elements of collective identity – shared understandings and local forms of organizing to help people cope – and noted that the more secure households tended to have better patterns of kin support. They also found other patterns of stratification, notably differences between the households of regular workers and the rest. But they emphasized that there was no sharp distinction at all between the culture and identity of people on the estate and those reported elsewhere in the wider society.

SUMMARY

- Images of inequality differ between those that focus on gradations and those that focus on divides.
- There is good evidence for increasing social polarization in the contemporary UK in terms of incomes and employment experience.
- Economic insecurity is worst for those on low incomes.
- Research suggests that income-related and work-related identities do not greatly differ between poor and better off people.

8 CONCLUSION

Income and work are important sources of identity. But how the connection works between what we do and have and who we are changes over time. Our central theme in this chapter has been that economic structures, such as the extent of inequality and the nature of employment (which themselves change over time), interact with our understandings of who we are, and of what we can do and be.

Categories such as social class, consumption cleavages and social polarization are used by social scientists to understand the links between inequality of incomes and wealth and people's identity and behaviour. But those categories are also sources of identity: we still label ourselves frequently in class terms. And they are also political ideas: taken up by government and the media, they influence how we see ourselves – not least by leading us to protest!

Another theme of the chapter has been the relative and relational nature of work and income as sources of identity. All of the main concepts we have introduced – poverty, inequality, social class, consumption cleavages, social polarization and social exclusion – are about the economic position of some people relative to others, and about how some people are represented relative to others. Another way of saying this is that work-related identities are socially produced: we cannot have such identities except in relation to others.

REFERENCES

Adonis, A. and Pollard, S. (1998) *A Class Act*, Harmondsworth, Penguin.

Banks, J., Dilnot, A. and Low, H. (1996) 'Patterns of financial wealth holding in the United Kingdom', in Hills, J. (1996).

Beresford, P. and Croft, S. (1995) 'It's our problem too! Challenging the exclusion of poor people from poverty discourse', *Critical Social Policy*, 44–5, pp.75–95.

Blackwell, T. and Seabrook, J. (1996) *Talking Work*, London, Faber and Faber.

Bourdieu, P. (1984) *Distinction: a Social Critique of the Judgement of Taste*, London, Routledge and Kegan Paul.

Bradley, H. (1996) *Fractured Identities*, Cambridge, Polity.

Brown, M. (1988) *Richard Branson: the Authorised Biography*, London, Headline.

Buck, N., Gershuny, J., Rose, D. and Scott, J. (1994) *Changing Households: Household Panel Study 1990–92*, University of Essex Centre on Micro-Social Change.

Crompton, R. (1998) *Class and Stratification* (2nd edn), Cambridge, Polity.

Dean, H. (1992) 'Poverty discourses and the disempowerment of the poor', *Critical Social Policy*, vol.35, pp.79–88.

Department of Social Security (DSS) (1997) *Households Below Average Incomes: A Statistical Analysis 1979–1994–5*, London, The Stationery Office.

Fernie, S. and Metcalfe, D. (1997) '(Not) hanging on the telephone: payment systems in the new sweatshops', Centre for Economic Performance, London School of Economics.

Gardiner, K. and Hills, J. (1999) 'Policy implications of new data on income mobility', *Economic Journal*, vol.109, no.453, February, pp.F91–F111.

Goldthorpe, J., Lockwood, D., Bechhoffer, F. and Platt, J. (1969) *The Affluent Worker: Industrial Attitudes and Behaviour*, Cambridge, Cambridge University Press.

Goodman, A., Johnson, P. and Webb, S. (1997) *Inequality in the UK*, Oxford, Oxford University Press.

Gregg, P. and Wadsworth, J. (1996) 'More work for fewer households?' in Hills, J. (1996).

Harkness, S., Machin, S. and Waldfogel, J. (1982) 'Female employment and changes in the share of women's earnings in total family income in Great Britain' in Hedges, N. and Beynon, H. (1982) *Born To Work*, London, Pluto Press.

Hills, J. (1995) *Joseph Rowntree Foundation Inquiry into Income and Wealth,* vols. 1 and 2, York, Joseph Rowntree Foundation.

Hills, J. (ed.) (1996) *New Inequalities: the Changing Distribution of Income and Wealth in the United Kingdom*, Cambridge, Cambridge University Press.

Hughes, G. and Fergusson, R. (eds) *Ordering Lives: Family, Work and Welfare*, London, Routledge/The Open University.

Hughes, J. (1984) 'The concept of class' in Anderson, R. and Sharrock, W. (eds) *Teaching Papers in Sociology*, London, Longman.

Jenkins, S. and Cowell, F. (1994) 'Dwarfs and giants in the 1980s: trends in the UK income distribution', *Fiscal Studies*, vol.15, no.1, pp.99–118.

Jordan, B., James, S., Kay, H. and Redley, M. (1992) *Trapped in Poverty? Labour Market Decisions in Low Income Households,* London, Routledge.

Jowell, R., Curtice, J., Park, A., Brook, L. and Ahrendt, D. (1995) *British Social Attitudes: the 12th Report* (1995/96 edn), Aldershot, Dartmouth Publishing.

Kempson, E. (1996) *Life on a Low Income*, York, Joseph Rowntree Foundation.

Lister, R. and Beresford, P. (1991) *Working Together Against Poverty: Involving Poor People in Action Against Poverty*, Open Seminar Project, University of Bradford.

Marx, K. and Engels, F. (1848/1986) *Manifesto of the Communist Party,* Moscow, Progress Publishers.

Marx, K. and Engels, F. (1983) *Collected Works*, vol.VI, Moscow, Progress Publishers.

Office of National Statistics (ONS) (1998) *Social Trends*, 28, (1998 edition) London, The Stationery Office.

Pakulski, J. and Waters, M. (1996) *The Death of Class*, London, Sage.

Pinch, S. (1993) 'Social polarisation: a comparison of evidence from Britain and the United States', *Environment and Planning*, vol.25, no.6, pp.779–95.

Saunders, P. (1984) 'Beyond housing classes: the sociological significance of private property rights in means of consumption', *International Journal of Urban and Regional Research*, vol.8, no.2, pp.202–27.

Scott, J. (1994) *Poverty and Wealth*, London, Longman.

Sen, A.K. (1981) *Poverty and Famines*, Oxford, Clarendon Press.

Taylor, P. and Bain, P. (1999) '"An assembly line in the head": work and employee relations in the call centre', *Industrial Relations Journal,* vol.30.

Tayor, S. (1998) 'Emotional labour and the new workplace' in Thompson, P.O. and Warhurst, C. (eds) *Workplaces of the Future*, London, Macmillan.

FURTHER READING

On inequality: John Hill's report to the Joseph Rowntree Foundation, *Inquiring into Income and Wealth*, vols. 1 and 2, is written for a general audience, and is very readable. It has a lot more on the income parade.

On social class: Rosemary Crompton's book, *Class and Stratification* (1998) is a fairly accessible survey.

On consumption: Edgell, S., Hetherington, K. and Warde, A. (eds) (1996) *Consumption Matters*, Oxford, Blackwell, can be recommended.

Harriet Bradley (1996) *Fractured Identities,* Cambridge, Polity, is a useful discussion of interrelationship between class and gender.

Gerth, H. and Mills, C.W. (1948) *From Max Weber,* London, Routledge – has excerpts from original texts by Weber and useful introductory commentary.

Karl Marx, *Communist Manifesto* – the real thing. Clear polemic which highlights key parts of Marxist mystique. A good read!

ANSWER TO ACTIVITY 3.2

A single person needed to earn £22,000 to get into the top tenth. A couple with children where only one adult was earning needed over £50,000. But a childless couple each earning £17,000 would get in.

Identity and nation

Montserrat Guibernau and David Goldblatt

Contents

1 INTRODUCTION

• •

> Identity is connected to a particular place ... by a feeling that you belong to that place. It's a place in which you feel comfortable, or at home, because part of how you define yourself is symbolized by certain qualities of that place.
>
> (Rose, 1990, p.89)

This chapter explores the relationships between our identities and the places that we come from. In fact, our identities and our home can be so intimately linked, so closely enmeshed and taken-for-granted, that it can be difficult to formalize and abstract those relationships, or reflect on precisely what qualities and what symbols best characterize home. Often, it takes a stranger, who has to learn the taken-for-granted cultures of a place, to expose them to scrutiny.

In 1991, the English writer Tony Parker went to Belfast. He stayed for over a year compiling a book of interviews with a wide range of the city's people. When trying to find a local assistant, whom he hoped might be personable, reliable, capable of keeping confidences and so on, the conversation soon turned to the issue of names.

> Of one, the first thing I'd been told was 'she'd be ideal, because her name's Teresa Green. So with a Catholic Christian name and a good sound Protestant surname, she could use either – which'd be a terrific advantage.' Someone recommending someone else said: 'She'd be most suitable: her name's Barbara you see, which is completely non-informative. In fact she's a Protestant but she's married to a Catholic – though she only says so when it's necessary. Another thing is they live in Stranmillis, which nowadays everybody knows of as a mixed Bohemian area, so that'd be a plus too.' Part of the description of a third person was: 'Her only drawback is she spent some of her childhood in Cheltenham, so she sometimes comes out with an English accent now and again without realising it.'
>
> (Parker, 1994, pp.2–3)

Reflecting on the experience Parker wrote: 'these introductory remarks about Christian and surnames, where people lived and what sort of accent they had, were all offering me an important glimpse, if only I'd been able to see it, of the totally different world I was to inhabit and become immersed in' (Parker, 1994, p.3). The Belfast of 1991 that Parker immersed himself in was a city where identity and place, nation and culture, were defining features of everyday life. Despite the progress of the peace process since Parker left Belfast, identity and its relationship to place (different parts of Belfast), to nation (Ireland and Britain), to religious tradition (Catholic or Protestant), and to politics (Nationalist and Unionist) still defines who you are and where you think you come from. Parker puts it like this.

however irrelevant and unimportant it seemed to me, a middle-class English agnostic pacifist, I soon and quickly started to learn what first and most mattered in Northern Ireland today – which is that no relationship can proceed unless certain basics are clarified to begin with. The first thing you need to know about someone as soon as you meet them – and they equally need to know about you – is whether each or both of you is Protestant or Catholic. To be 'neither' is not sufficient ...

The need for knowledge of someone's present faith or antecedents isn't for the purpose of expressing empathy or antagonism, but purely so that any following conversation can continue with greater ease. Once you know whether you share common background, or you do not, thereafter you can avoid saying the wrong thing, or wrong word, to unwittingly cause offence.

Anyone born and brought up in Northern Ireland can do this effortlessly, practised since birth: almost by extra-sensory perception, it seems at times.

(Parker, 1994, pp.3–4)

ACTIVITY 4.1

Read Parker's description of two early encounters in Belfast (Reading 4.1) and take a look at the map of Belfast (Figure 4.1) which shows the distribution of the Catholic population at the time.

What issues of identity are being signalled by the speakers?

What is the connection being drawn by the estate agent between identity and place in west Belfast?

Tony Parker: 'May the Lord in His mercy be kind to Belfast'

Chemist's shop assistant

– Just the one fillum you want to have developed and printed is it sir? With pleasure, no problem, it'll be back here for you tomorrow. We don't process them here on the premises ourselves, we send them away. They go either to Johnson and Hunter or Collins and Sullivan, which would you prefer? Well it's just as you please sir: they both take exactly the same length of time, they'll be back here by ten o'clock. No they're the same price, there's no difference. Johnson and Hunter give you a free fillum with them – but then of course so do Collins and Sullivan too. Well it's for you to say which one you'd like sir. Really no preference? Then we'll send them to Johnson and Hunter shall we, OK?

Estate agent

– What area were you looking for rented accommodation in sir? Have you any preference for any particular part of the city? Would you want to be central, or on the outskirts perhaps? The Malone Road of course, that's a good area, handy for the south of the city. Or the north, or the east perhaps, would you fancy something in that direction, say towards Holywood which is a nice area? Can you give me an idea what sort of price you had in mind? Well I'm sure we could find you something suitable at around that figure. I'd imagine something on the east side of the Lough – maybe even towards Bangor if you don't mind a fifteen or twenty minute journey in. What about facilities nearby, would you want it to be handy for a golf club say, or a particular church? No? Well then I'm sure we can offer you several places to choose from. Definitely let's say on the east and to the north, that's where most of our properties tend to be anyway.

Source: Parker, 1994, pp.10, 7

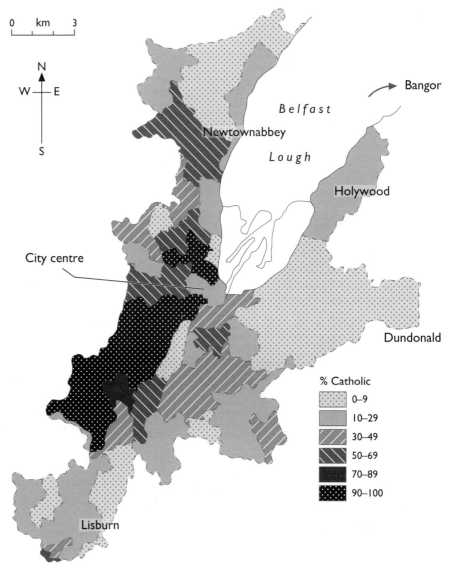

FIGURE 4.1   Distribution of Catholic population in Belfast, 1991
Source: Boal, 1995, p.29

COMMENT

These were Parker's own reflections on the conversations, reflections that show how he had begun to learn to read the cultures, symbols and signs of identity and place in Belfast.

[CHEMIST'S SHOP ASSISTANT]

An almost perfect example ... of an utterly clueless Englishman being baffled by an everyday situation, to the extent of not even being aware he was in it. Only several weeks later did the penny suddenly drop.

Johnson and Hunter are of course at once recognisable merely by their name as being Protestant. Just as Collins and Sullivan are Catholic, as surely all but the dimmest of the dim would be expected to recognise. So naturally, if you're Protestant you'll want your fillum developed and printed by Protestants, and by Catholics if you're Catholic. Naturally. You wouldn't want to give patronage and financial support to the other side.

When at last it became clear I didn't know this, being not only an ignoramus but probably an unbeliever as well, the young woman had to make the decision herself.

And of course, because of which she chose, apparently randomly but on reflection most certainly not, it was obvious what she was.

[ESTATE AGENT]

Obviously the estate agent was Protestant and presumed I would be too, coming from England and coming to him. Hence there was no mention of property in west Belfast, which is almost entirely Catholic. There was still a slight doubt in his mind at the beginning though.

The Malone Road is, it's true, 'a good area', and a popular one for mainly professional middle-class people. It used to be almost entirely Protestant, but now has Catholic residents as well: by the time you're high enough up the social ladder to want property there, your financial standing counts for more than your religious affiliation. If I had been Catholic I would have known that, and expressed at least an initial interest, just as an aware Protestant would know of Holywood as 'a nice area'. The large Catholic church there was burned down in somewhat mysterious circumstances a year or two ago.

Bangor is middle-class respectability personified, or likes to think of itself as such. It has a yachting marina built with financial help from the EEC. 'Facilities ... a golf club or a particular church' was a final baiting of a hook to try and learn a little more.

(Parker, 1994, pp.17–18, 14)

ACTIVITY 4.2

Before you read the rest of this chapter, take a few minutes to answer the question: 'where do you come from?' Then write down a few notes on it.

Think what is specific about the place you come from: language, sports, landscape, famous monuments, a particular type of music, a particular type of weather. What qualities, if any, characterize the place?

Have you answered by giving the name of a village, town or a city, a particular region, a nation? Whatever your answer it is likely that you define yourself and your identity, at least in part, through connections to a particular place. It may have been a very easy and unambiguous question for you. On the other hand, some of you may have had doubts or uncertainties about the question 'where do you come from?' Have you, for example, said, 'I'm British but I come from Pakistan', or 'I come from Aberdeen and I'm British', or 'I come from Aberdeen and I'm Scottish', or 'Scottish and British'. The same kind of diversity could be found in England and Wales as well. In Belfast, in 1991, the range of options and the freedom of choice of identities would have been more restricted. As Parker noted, neutrality was not an option. But all the examples suggest that while the place where you come from usually plays a key role in defining your identity, there is no simple equation between place of birth, place of residence, official citizenship, and personal identity. Has the relationship between place and identity in the UK always been ambiguous? For most of us, who hold a single passport, our official national identity is usually clear. In the UK we are British. But as we know from the earlier chapters in this book, times and identities change.

In the last couple of decades, people's identification with Britishness and indeed the content of what it is to be British does appear increasingly fragile and uncertain. The rise of a more robust and entrenched Scottish national identity has been paralleled by a strengthening sense of Welsh national identity. Both of these national identities are contested, and many of the Scots and Welsh wish to cultivate their distinct national identities while retaining their sense of Britishness and rejecting the idea of a separate, independent Scottish or Welsh state. Yet there can be little doubt that these national identities are stronger, more confident and widespread than they have been at any point in the twentieth century. In Northern Ireland, a significant proportion of the population have always seen themselves as Irish rather than British.

Alongside this internal fragmentation of Britain, three other changes have made the idea of Britain and Britishness more uncertain in the last few decades. First, some of the key institutions of Britishness, institutions that have symbolized the nation, have been transformed. The British Empire has evaporated and the British monarchy's institutional popularity has plummeted. Second, Britain has joined the European Union. At an official, if not at a popular or informal level, we are all Europeans. For some, this is unproblematic, even to be welcomed. For others, membership of the European Union and the prospect of further European integration is a profound threat to the maintenance of a distinct British national identity. Third, the demand for labour generated by the economic growth of the 1950s and 1960s saw a great wave of migration to Britain from Britain's former colonies in the Caribbean and the Indian sub-continent. Although concentrated in England and its large cities, Britain has acquired a significant indigenous black presence in every county. For some, this cultural diversity is welcomed. For others, the meaning of Britishness has been destabilized.

The tasks of this chapter are to explore in more detail why British identity may be more uncertain than it has been in the past and what some of the consequences of that uncertainty might be. While earlier chapters have focused on the role of biological, social and economic structures in shaping identities, this chapter focuses on the role of culture in the making and unmaking of national identities.

In what ways have we already touched on the role of culture – the web of meanings, symbols and signs, ideas and beliefs, within which we live – in creating and sustaining identities?

Look back to the Belfast example:

- names, knowledge of and preferences for certain residential patterns, accents and modes of speech are markers of identity.

We begin, in Section 2, by clarifying some of the key social science concepts and arguments; defining the ideas of nation, nation-state and nationalism. In Section 3 we put some of these ideas to work, looking at the historical and *cultural* origins of the United Kingdom (a nation-state) and Britishness (a national identity). In Section 4 we move on from the creation of nations and national identities to the role of culture in sustaining and reproducing those identities. In particular we look at the role of national symbols and rituals. In Section 5 we put these ideas and concepts to work by looking at the case of Scotland, asking why it should be that Scottish national identity appears to be challenging, even replacing Britishness as a primary source of identity amongst some Scots. Finally, in Section 6, we explore the consequences of this, and the other historical changes outlined above, for England and the English. For if any identity has become more uncertain and more problematic, it is probably not Britishness, but Englishness.

2 NATIONS, NATION-STATES AND NATIONAL IDENTITY

2.1 What is a nation?

ACTIVITY 4.3

Which of the following, if any, are nations and which are nation-states?

Britain

England

Ireland

Northern Ireland

The Republic of Ireland

Scotland

Wales

The United Kingdom

COMMENT

- The only nation-states in the list are the United Kingdom and the Republic of Ireland.

- England, Scotland and Wales are commonly thought of as nations, but there is no English state, Scottish state, or Welsh state, at present.

- Northern Ireland, in formal constitutional terms, is part of the United Kingdom, but very few people would consider it a nation or describe themselves as Northern Irish. Some refer to it as a province, others as the six counties, others as Ulster. Some people who live there consider themselves Irish, others consider themselves British, and some see their identity as Ulster men or women.

- Some people consider Ireland (the whole island and its people) as a nation, irrespective of the border. Many Northern Irish Protestants would bitterly contest this.

- Some people consider Britain and its people (that is, the UK without Northern Ireland) to be a nation; some would contest this.

The point of this activity is not to answer the initial question definitively, but to show how complex and contested the idea of a nation is, and to show how there is no easy or automatic fit between nations and nation-states. To unpack this issue, we need some basic definitions. Let's begin with the idea of the **state**. For our purposes the state is a cluster of institutions which lay claim to ultimate legal and moral authority over a given territory and whose claim is usually backed up by the monopoly of legal force and legal violence within that territory. In the UK today, the state is made up of the government, parliament, Whitehall and its ministries, national quangos, local government, the army and police. We use the term the UK state as a shorthand for these governing institutions.

If you look at a political map of the world today you will see clearly-marked borders that separate states from each other. However, the existence of clearly-marked and agreed borders is actually a fairly recent innovation. For most of human history, whatever the claims of states and their rulers, borders have been indistinct and unmapped. The authority of states and their monopoly of force, rather than being uniform over a territory, have tended to be strong at the centre but peter-out into ungovernable border lands and

State
The cluster of institutions which claim ultimate law-making authority over a territory, and claim the monopoly on legitimate use of coercion and violence.

FIGURE 4.2
Europe, 1000 AD

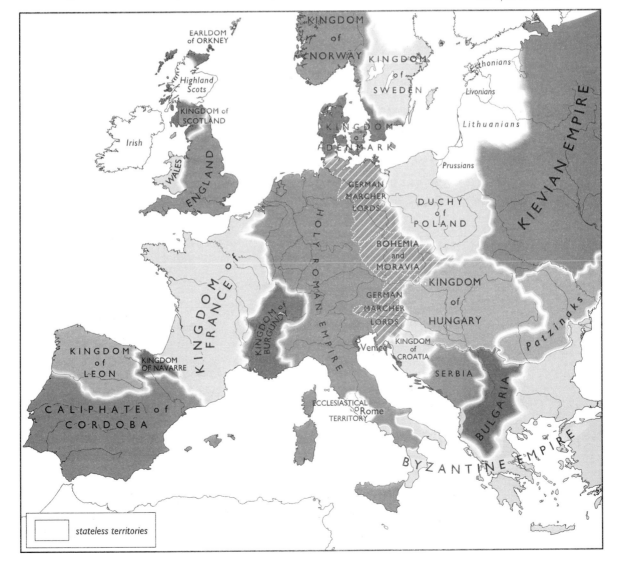

stateless territories

peripheries. This was true of great imperial states like Rome, and of feudal states like England in the fifteenth century when the rule of law rarely extended to the far north of England, for example. **Nation-states**, which we see represented on today's political maps – with fixed borders and uniform internal rule – have only been created in the last few centuries in Europe and even more recently in most of the rest of the world.

Nation-state
A state which possesses external fixed, known, demarcated borders, and possesses an internal uniformity of rule.

What then is the relationship between nations and nation-states? One claim has been that all people living within the fixed boundaries of a nation-state and under its uniform rule constitute a single community of fate, bound together in a common destiny by allegiance to a single set of state institutions. This appears to work for France, for example. France is the nation-state, and the French are the nation of people who live within its boundaries and under its rule; although the Bretons in the north of France, and the Basques who live near the Spanish border might have something to say about this. This simple equation between nation and nation-state soon breaks down once you look at

FIGURE 4.3
Europe, 1999 AD

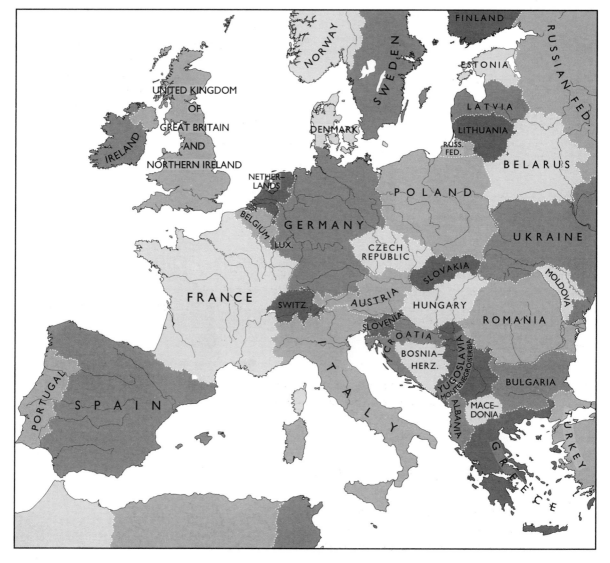

a wider range of examples. In the case of Ireland, the island is divided into the Republic of Ireland, which achieved independence from Britain in 1921, and part of the UK nation-state: Northern Ireland. There are, however, many Catholics living in Northern Ireland who consider themselves part of the Irish nation but who live under the rule of the UK state. Alternatively, Scottish or Welsh nationalists consider themselves to be members of the Scottish or Welsh nation, but live under the rule of the UK state.

These conflicts and differences exist because, in the end, the nation-state is a political and legal entity, but **nations** are cultural entities. They are communities of people who feel they possess the same identity by virtue of shared cultures, histories, languages; and the geography of those communities does not necessarily correspond to the geography of political borders. In this context we can understand **nationalism** as both a psychological and political phenomenon. On the one hand nationalism is a psychological and emotional attachment to a nation, a sense of belonging and identity. But, more often than not, this emotional attachment to a community of fate has become entangled with a political project – the idea that a nation should govern itself, that it should acquire a nation-state of its own which can protect and nurture the interests and identity of that nation. It is this, in part, which distinguishes nations from other shared cultures and identities (Guibernau, 1998).

If it is the case that nation-states are fairly recent innovations whose external borders and internal rule have only been secured over many years and usually through the outcome of wars, are nations recent innovations too?

Nation
A named people who acknowledge a shared solidarity and identity by virtue of a shared culture, history and territorial homeland.

Nationalism
An emotive identification with a nation and a political project to secure an independent nation-state for a nation.

If you were able to ask an East Anglian peasant of the thirteenth century 'are you English?', or a Highland crofter of the same era, 'are you Scottish?', would they have replied, unambiguously, yes?

We cannot say for certain. There are almost no written records of the allegiances and identities of these people. But more likely than not they would have either said no, or only acknowledged their Englishness or Scottishness as one very minor and ambiguous element amongst a whole host of other identities. They would be much more likely to identify themselves in relation to a village or a region, or as part of a particular family, or even as Christians and part of Christendom.

To get a clearer sense of the meaning and origins of nations and national identities we need to take a look at some of the attempts of social scientists to describe and account for these phenomena.

2.2 Social scientists on nations

One of the most influential accounts of the origins of nations has been provided by the anthropologist and philosopher Ernest Gellner (1983). In Gellner's view nations have only come into being with the advent of

Industrialization
The processes initiated in a society by the introduction of fossil fuel energy, complex productive machinery and transportation, and a shift from agriculture to manufacturing.

modernization in general and **industrialization** in particular. In Gellner's terms, modernization refers to a complex and interrelated set of social changes that transform agrarian societies and their simple patterns of hierarchy and religious integration into complex industrial, secular societies, with large-scale bureaucratic states, and complex and shifting patterns of hierarchy and integration. Gellner argues that all modernizing societies require the development of a common culture and a common language if they are not to disintegrate. The complex division of labour that emerges in industrializing economies requires people to possess a simple, shared medium of communication to function effectively. Modern bureaucracies require that the populace can read the forms it produces and the directives it issues. Above all, such complex and potentially fragmentary societies require shared ideas and meanings that link people together into a common project. All of this requires the mass education of the population. As a consequence, any state that is undergoing modernization or wants to initiate modernization and develop massive bureaucratic systems must create a homogenizing, centrally determined mass education system which effectively imposes a single language and a single culture from above. Minority, folk and peripheral languages or cultures are effectively squeezed out of the system or are actively quashed to create a single mass national culture. From this springs a single nation and national identity. In short, nations are not ancient or timeless communities of blood or culture, but a modern invention that fits the functional and cultural requirements of modern societies.

The political scientist and historian Benedict Anderson also locates the origins of nations and nationalism in the processes of modernization, but while Gellner focuses on industrialism and the educational system, Anderson is also concerned with more informal systems of literacy and the interactions of nations and nation-states with each other (Anderson, 1983). Anderson's starting point is the idea of the nation as an *imagined community*.

> It is imagined because the members of even the smallest nation will never know most of their fellow members, meet them, or ever hear of them ... The nation is imagined as limited because even the largest of them, encompassing perhaps a billion living human beings, has finite, if elastic, boundaries, beyond which lie other nations. No nation imagines itself coterminous with mankind ... It is imagined as sovereign because the concept was born in an age in which Enlightenment and Revolution were destroying the legitimacy of the divinely-ordained, hierarchical dynastic realm ... nations dream of being free ... it is imagined as a community, because, regardless of the actual inequality and exploitation that may prevail ... the nation is always conceived as a deep, horizontal comradeship.
>
> (Anderson, 1983, pp.15–16)

Of course, in any kind of society that operates beyond face-to-face interaction, some kind of imagining is required (see the discussion of G.H. Mead and the imagining of the other in Chapter 1, Section 3.1). What distinguishes nations as imagined communities is the type of imagining that goes on. As the quote above illustrates, the nation, in modern times, has been imagined as a *limited* community that exists in a sea of other nations and other peoples from which it sharply demarcates itself. It also imagines itself as a community of *self-rule* as sovereign, possessing its own fixed and bordered nation-state. Modern nations, according to Anderson, spring from the emergence of new communication media like printing and the telegraph system and their combination with free-market capitalism; processes which began as early as the seventieth century in Europe. These new systems of communication allowed people, over much wider geographical areas than before, to imagine themselves as part of the same community of fate. The emergence of capitalism and of independent publishers, for example, meant that the control of culture and communication was taken out of the hands of churches and governments. When combined with a shared language that was clearly distinct from others, and a shared culture across classes, the preconditions for the development of modern national identities were met. The nation-states that emerged have done so in the context of the international system of states that surround them. Drawing the boundaries between nation-states has rarely taken the form of peaceable negotiations, more often than not it has required prolonged political and military conflict to secure borders.

A third approach to the origins of nations is exemplified by Anthony D. Smith (1986, 1995). While Smith acknowledges the importance of industrialization, mass literacy, the international state system and so on, he argues that you cannot create nations out of nothing. There has to be some pre-existing community, bound by language or culture or religion from which a modern nation can be forged. Therefore, Smith starts with the concept of an ethnie or **ethnic community**. He argues that most contemporary European nations find their roots in ethnic communities which began to take shape in the Middle Ages. Thus, prior to the formation of modern nations, we can find traces and elements of ethnic communities – like the Welsh (with their shared language) or the Scots (with their allegiance to a feudal state distinct from the English) – which formed the raw materials from which modern nations were created. For Smith, what separates a loosely connected ethnic community from a nation is possession of: '(1) an historic territory, or homeland; (2) common myths and historical memories; (3) a common, mass public culture; (4) common legal rights and duties for all members; and (5) a common economy with territorial mobility for members' (Smith, 1986). While (3), (4) and (5) can all be created by Gellner's modernizing state, or Anderson's print capitalism, it is far more difficult to invent (1) or (2) out of nowhere and out of nothing.

Ethnic community
A named but loosely bound group of people whose shared identity is related to culture, history and/or language, but whose relationship to territory and statehood is more indeterminate than a nation.

SUMMARY

- Nation-states are states with known fixed external boundaries and uniform patterns of internal rule. They have only come into being in the last few hundred years.

- Nations are cultural entities, consisting of groups of people from across the social scale who consider themselves part of the same community of fate, bound by shared histories, cultures and/or language.

- Some nation-states may contain more than one nation. Nations may be split between many nation-states.

- Nationalism is both a psychological and emotive identification with one's nation and a political project that seeks political self-determination for that nation often in the form of an independent nation-state.

- Gellner, Anderson and Smith offer distinct accounts of the origins and character of nations. Gellner focuses on modernization, industrialization and an imposed mass national culture. Anderson focuses on print capitalism and imagined communities from below. Smith focuses on the ethnic origins of nations and their subsequent acquisition of common histories and cultures.

3 WHAT IS BRITAIN?: CREATING NATIONAL IDENTITIES

Whatever the differences between the three accounts of the origins of nations outlined in Section 2, they all agree that a common culture of shared meanings is a necessary precondition for the construction and experience of national identity. But just as you cannot invent nations out of nothing and nowhere, so common cultures and shared meanings cannot be understood separately from the political, economic and military affairs of a society. In this section we look at the broad social context in which a national identity – British national identity – arose.

So who are the British? If you had asked the question of anyone in the seventeenth century in the lands that are now Britain, you would, amongst a small educated elite, have been told of some of the peoples that populated the land before the Romans who called themselves Britons. Since the Romans left, in the fifth century AD, the British Isles has absorbed a large number of different migrant groups and invaders. No case then, or now, could be made for a single, original, authentic group of Britons.

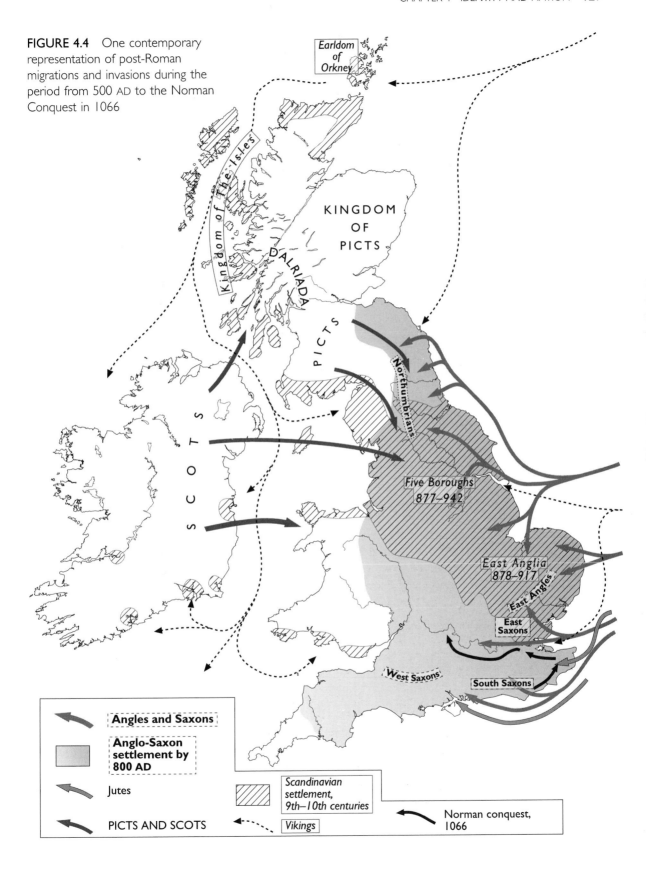

FIGURE 4.4 One contemporary representation of post-Roman migrations and invasions during the period from 500 AD to the Norman Conquest in 1066

The political and cultural map of the British Isles has been shaped and reshaped by successive patterns of migration, invasion, war, and alliance amongst ruling aristocratic dynasties and noble houses. The English monarchy (of Norman origin) first subdued the Welsh-speaking aristocracy in the twelfth and thirteenth centuries and then formally incorporated the principality into its realm in 1536 – a realm which included large parts of France for most of the previous 400 years. But the combination of these two feudal realms did not constitute Britain. Scotland had existed as a separate feudal kingdom for centuries. At various times it had fallen under the control of the English Crown, but had maintained its independence since the decisive wars of the fourteenth century. Since 1603 Scotland and England were ruled by the same Stuart dynasty but as separate kingdoms. Ireland, in so far as anyone controlled the island, was treated as a separate colony of England and contained a complex mix of Celtic tribal clan and chieftain systems overlain by an implanted Anglo-French Norman aristocracy whose presence dated back to the early twelfth century.

What changed the map, and demanded the invention of Britain and Britishness, was the 1707 Act of Union, passed by the Westminster parliament it linked Scotland to England and Wales and announced there would be 'one United Kingdom by the name of Great Britain'. In the terms we outlined in Section 2, there was an embryonic British nation-state, but no British nation. In fact, it would be hard to argue that, in modern terms at any rate, an English, Scottish or Welsh nation existed. All three were sharply divided by religion, language and dialect. Beyond the confines of aristocratic and merchant cultures, people from Cumbria and Cornwall, the South Wales villages and mountains of North Wales, or the Highlands and lowlands of Scotland would have been barely able to communicate with each other. As Linda Colley (1992, p.17) puts it: 'Great Britain in 1707 was much less a trinity of three self-contained and self-conscious nations than a patchwork in which uncertain areas of Welshness, Scottishness and Englishness were cut across by strong regional attachments, and scored over again by loyalties to village, town, family and landscape'. Out of this unlikely hybrid nature a sense of British national identity was invented and created around five key pillars.

1 Geography

   Britain is an island. This gave it clear, unmistakable boundaries, unlike most of the emerging states in Europe. However, this external marker did not guarantee internal unity or the creation of a common culture.

2 Religion

   Although significant Catholic communities continued to exist and practice on mainland Britain and Catholicism remained the dominant popular religion in Ireland, Protestantism was the central shared characteristic of the three national components of Great Britain. It was also the Protestant churches and their use of vernacular English for services and the Bible that began the process of creating a more homogenous, island-wide English language. While the churches of England, Scotland and Wales remained independent from each other these divisions paled into insignificance against their collective differences from Catholicism – differences that had been deepened by the revolutionary events of the Reformation, the dissolution of the monasteries and the European wars of religion in the seventeenth century.

3 War

The importance of Protestantism as a shared British identity was entrenched by the experience of war, both international and civil. In the eighteenth and early nineteenth centuries the main threats to the existence of Britain as a Protestant nation-state came from Catholic forces. In 1715 and 1745 remnants of the Catholic Stuart dynasty and Highland clans mounted unsuccessful Scots-based rebellions against the Hanoverian Protestant monarchy. In the wider world, Britain fought a series of European and global imperial wars with Catholic France – its main global competitor. The Seven Years War (1756–63) was fought out in North America, the Caribbean and Europe, and led to the expulsion of France from most of its North American possessions. The American War of Independence (1776–81), between Britain and her American colonies, saw large-scale French intervention on the side of the colonists. These conflicts culminated in the titanic struggles of the Napoleonic wars of the early nineteenth century. The financial and human sacrifices of these wars, and the global British dominance they helped secure, defined and embedded a distinct idea of Britishness; primarily, but not exclusively, amongst the elites that staffed the British state, navy and army, and the men of property whose taxes paid for them.

4 Empire, land and commerce

If external threats helped bind the British elite together, it was the success of Empire, land and commerce that did most to internally unite them. English aristocratic families acquired Scottish, Welsh and Irish estates in this era, and some (although few) Scottish and Welsh landowners bought or married into the English elite. The economic and cultural dominance of the English meant that many of the Irish and Scots gentry, in particular, made their way through alternative routes provided by the British state. Both Scots and Irish were over represented in the officer class of the army, and amongst imperial explorers, administrators and successful imperial merchants. Success in the wars against France, acquisition of the global Empire and early industrialization helped create fabulous economic and political opportunities. The elites of England, Scotland and Wales were bound together in a common project of imperial conquest, administration and trade.

5 Monarchy

In their different ways, geography, war, religion and Empire were the structural conditions within which a successful British national identity could emerge, providing real material interests and opportunities that could bind people together; but national identities need cultural content and symbols through which a community can be imagined and represented to itself. This final pillar of British national identity provided those symbols. The ruling dynasty of the era was the Protestant Hanoverians, whose accession to the throne was based on theology rather than their ethnic origins. The first three Georges continued to speak German and retained extensive residences in Hanover. Their political and social standing was badly eroded by the loss of the American colonies and a deliberate effort was made by the monarchy and its allies to reinvent itself as British rather than Hanoverian, and to provide the dominant symbols and rituals of the British nation. It was only in the middle decades of the eighteenth century that a national anthem – 'God Save the King' – was acquired. Royal-sponsored institutions – like the British Museum – were created. The Union flag followed even later. The details of this history need not concern us here. The key point is that the cultural symbols of the British nation were sponsored by and devised around the monarchy. To be French, after the revolution, was to be a male citizen of the Republic. To be British was to be a male land-owning subject of the Crown.

None the less, even in the early nineteenth century, the creation of Britain was far from complete. There remained entrenched pockets of Scottish and Welsh identity, Gaelic and Welsh speakers, republicans who rejected the monarchy, and a great mass of people, often illiterate, identifying only with their narrow localities. Above all, Britain was never a union of equals and Britishness was always more closely aligned with Englishness, and landed aristocratic Englishness, than it was a genuine hybrid of the English and Celts or a mass, popular nationalism.

ACTIVITY 4.4

Look back to the accounts of nations and national identity in Section 2.2. What light might they shed on the account of the origins of Britain outlined above?

COMMENT _____

- Gellner's work suggests that national identities only become mass rather than elite phenomena with the onset of industrialization. The account above only concerns the formation of an elite British national identity. It would take the demands of industrialization and the growth of the British state in the nineteenth century for ideas of Britishness to permeate down to all classes in society.

- Anderson's account of national identity suggests that it takes mass literacy (again a late nineteenth-century phenomenon) to make a mass imagined community possible, but because his account is separated from industrialization, etc., it can be applied to the more restricted male land-owning nation that was Britain in the eighteenth century. A common British elite culture was fused around a print-based English language culture. Anderson's point about the formation of nations in the context of war and an international state system is confirmed by the account of Britain.

- Smith's model of national identity reminds us that despite the real importance of Britishness as a source of identity in this era, older communities and cultures continued to persist, which Britishness could never eradicate.

We will return to Britishness in Section 6. But before doing so, we want to look in more detail at how, under the right circumstances, cultural inventions and traditions can act as a key source of national identity.

SUMMARY

- The British nation-state, created by the 1707 Act of Union, preceded the creation of a British nation.
- Prior to the nineteenth century, Britishness was created around the pillars of geography, Protestantism, war, Empire and monarchy.
- Britishness was, initially, primarily an elite identity, dominated by Englishness.
- Britishness became a more secure mass national identity with the advent of industrialization and mass literacy.
- Pre-existing ethnic identities and allegiances never completely disappeared.

4 SUSTAINING NATIONS: CULTURE AND NATIONAL IDENTITY

In Sections 2 and 3 we have focused on the definition and creation of nations and, in the case of Britain, we have looked at the ways in which war, religion and culture combined to create a sense of Britishness. In this section we move from these large-scale events to some of the more detailed cultural mechanisms that sustain and reproduce a sense of national identity.

ACTIVITY 4.5

At the beginning of this chapter you were asked the question: 'where do you come from?'

Return to the description you made of the place where you come from and think of some occasions on which you may have felt a sense of solidarity with people who come from the same place as you.

Write down a brief description of these occasions.

COMMENT _____

You may have experienced a sense of solidarity towards some of your fellow country men and women who have suffered an accident abroad.

You may recall a sense of solidarity amongst supporters of a football team.

Depending on your age, you may recall a sense of solidarity felt by yourself or some close relatives or friends who fought in the Second World War.

_____

These are all examples of how a sense of common national identity can engender feelings of solidarity amongst its members. That solidarity is based upon the consciousness of forming a group; outsiders are strangers. A sense of national identity and internal solidarity requires that we draw distinctions between ourselves and others. But what 'we' are cannot be sustained by opposition and difference alone. The cultural construction of national identities also requires more specific content. That content can be provided and reinforced by national symbols and national rituals.

4.1 Symbols and national identity

Meanings about national identity are produced through symbolic systems; through images, stories, flags, styles of dress, uniforms, all the different components of a community's culture and its traditions. A symbol is a sign that stands for something else; something that it signifies (see Chapter 1, Section 3.1 on symbols). The flag is perhaps one of the most useful examples of a signifier of national identity. A whole set of meanings is condensed into one sign which is used to represent the nation-state.

_____

Take the example of the Union Jack. This is a sign, but what does it stand for? What do you associate with this flag?

_____

There are several possibilities. It could be the British Empire, the British people, British traditions, the Queen and parliament, British fashion week, Britpop or right-wing extremists. Your association might be positive – the flag represents the best of British: fair play and independence – or your association might be negative – for example, seeing the Union Jack as a sign of British oppression of peoples overseas.

FIGURE 4.5 Buckingham Palace flies the flag

FIGURE 4.6 British fashion week

The meaning of a symbol is not fixed. Symbols can be read in different ways, particularly when accompanied by other images and narratives. Roland Barthes in *Mythologies* (1972) describes a picture in the magazine *Paris Match*, showing a black soldier in a French uniform saluting the French flag with his eyes uplifted. Barthes argues that this image has been chosen by the magazine to show that France is a great empire and that all her sons, whether black or white, faithfully serve under her flag. That there is no better answer to an 'alleged colonialism than the zeal shown ... in serving his so-called oppressors' (Barthes, 1972, p.116).

The flag is only one symbol of the nation. As we have seen in this chapter there are others. The five pillars identified in Section 3 all involve representations of what it means to be British. Britain may be a relatively recent invention historically, but it is from the reconstruction of the past through stories, and symbols of island-living, of war and of Empire that an idea of Britishness in the present is re-created.

4.2 Rituals and national identity

Human memory is short lived and relatively limited. The same is true of the collective memories that sustain collective national identities. National identities need to be upheld and reaffirmed at regular intervals. Rituals play a crucial role here: however, what exactly is a ritual? Its most common usage is associated with religious services and practices and it is precisely this connection that the French sociologist Émile Durkheim explored in his book *The Elementary Forms of the Religious Life* (1915). Durkheim argued that despite considerable differences in their content there are few formal or functional differences between religious and national, secular ceremonies and rituals; their intentions, their consequences and the processes employed to attain the same results are remarkably similar.

Durkheim argued that religion embodies and represents the collective values which underpin a society's unity. Religious ceremonies served to reinforce collective values and reaffirm a sense of community among individuals. He suggested that religious rituals took people away from the routine of daily existence and transported them into a sacred realm. Although the 'old gods' were dead, Durkheim suggested that nations needed the cohesion and unity which such rituals and their sense of the sacred could create. Such rituals would clearly be attractive to those who seek to forge national identity. National heroes and national celebrations of their lives could take on the sacred character of the religious celebrations.

In the UK, the state, monarchy and Church of England are closely linked: the Queen is head of state and of the church which together form the core of most British national rituals. Drawing on the language of religious ritual and the presence of church leaders, royal and state occasions are used to confirm the 'British way of life' and the public are invited to participate, primarily through television.

Can you think of other examples of British national rituals or of the nation to which you belong?

Which aspects of national identity are being celebrated or remembered? Are all members of the population included? Do different groups treat rituals in different ways?

Remembrance Sunday is just one example of a ritual occasion which constructs a particular view of belonging to the nation. Remembrance day is not just about remembering the past, it creates one view of the nation in the present and makes the experience of war part of British identity. The public representation of war, for example through television coverage of the laying of wreaths at the Cenotaph in Whitehall and the British Legion's Poppy Appeal, draws people into the *imagined community* of Britain; a Britain whose national identity is closely connected to military endeavours with all

FIGURE 4.7   The Cenotaph, Whitehall on Remembrance Sunday

the associations of heroism, self-sacrifice and honour. When the UK fights wars, such as in the Falklands or the Gulf War where it was part of an international force, it is the British army, not an army from the UK or its constituent nations, which is involved. Remembrance Sunday is one of the public rituals which re-creates and reproduces this history of a united Britain upon which we draw on other occasions, such as at times of military action against other nations.

SUMMARY

- Symbols and rituals are key factors in the construction of national identity. They establish the boundaries between those who belong and those who do not belong to the group.

- Symbols and rituals can strengthen the consciousness of forming a community and to be effective they have to be invoked and repeated at regular intervals.

5 FRAGMENTING NATIONS: SCOTTISH NATIONALISM AND NATIONAL IDENTITY

The incorporation of the Scottish parliament into the Westminster parliament was the political keystone of the Union on which a superstructure of Britishness – cultural, imperial and institutional – was created. Nearly 300 years later that keystone is not only dislodged but transformed. The Scottish parliament of the seventeenth century was elected on a tiny franchise of male landowners, it met rarely and made legislation sporadically. It barely scrutinized the executive branch of government – the Crown. In September 1997, the Scots, by a significant majority (74 per cent for establishing the Scottish parliament and 63 per cent to give it tax-varying powers) voted in favour of establishing a very different Scottish parliament. The first elections to the parliament, on a universal suffrage and partly proportional system, took place in Spring 1999. Members of the Scottish parliament are responsible for legislation on a wide range of issues (notable exclusions are foreign policy and defence, macroeconomic policy, and abortion) and have considerable powers of executive scrutiny. They nominate a candidate for First Minster who will normally be the leader of the party able to command the majority support of the Scottish parliament. The post of First Minster supersedes the Scottish Secretary of State appointed by Westminster and takes executive control of the Scottish Office and its considerable budget and bureaucracy.

It has been a long and complex process towards self-determination for Scotland. From the moment the Union was forged Scots have divided over its merits and someone or other has always been defending the Union, calling for a measure of constitutional reform or home rule or demanding an independent Scottish state. For most of Scottish history the weight of opinion and power has lain with the advocates of the Union. However, on a number of occasions the balance has shifted. In the years before and immediately after the First World War home rule bills for Scotland were tabled at Westminster, but these were blocked by the emergency of war, unionist opposition and Westminster indifference. In 1919 radical socialist demands flared up for an independent Scottish workers' republic, but these were doused by more coercive means. The balance of opinion and power did not shift again until the 1960s with the emergence of significant support for constitutional reform within the Union in the Scottish labour movement and the emergence of a revitalized Scottish Nationalist Party (SNP) arguing for independence. Following a decade of debate and pressure the Labour government called a referendum in 1979. The Scots voted in favour of establishing a Scottish Assembly. However, no assembly was created because the referendum required that at least 40 per cent of the registered electorate should vote in favour. Only 32.9 per cent of the electorate actually did so (overviews of Scottish history drawn from Lynch, 1992; Marr, 1992; Harvie, 1998).

Unlike during the inter-war years, the calls for both constitutional reform and national independence did not disappear. They grew stronger and were insistent in all political parties except the Scottish Conservatives and were more widespread across Scotland, both socially and geographically. In 1988 the Scottish Constitutional Convention was initiated. This network of Scotland's political, administrative, cultural, educational and other elites drew representatives from Scottish Labour and Liberal Democrats, churches, trade unions and other civic groups. The SNP, after considering joining, remained outside, although dissident nationalists were represented. In 1995 the convention published a plan for a Scottish parliament which had the backing of a broad swathe of Scottish public opinion. However, the Conservative government of the time was implacably opposed to the measures and it required the defeat of the Conservatives in the 1997 General Election to unlock the process. The Labour Party, who had been dependent on Scottish votes and MPs in the 1980s and 1990s, was firmly committed to a new referendum on a Scottish parliament.

This very truncated account of the creation of the new Scottish parliament clearly begs some questions, not least about Scottish national identity and the progress of Scottish nationalism. We want to look at three.

- If the Scottish nation-state went south with the 1707 Union, what happened to the Scottish nation in the meantime? Why did it appear so disinclined to rule itself?

- What, if anything, has the changing character of Scottish national identity contributed to tipping the political balance of opinion from the Union to either constitutional reform or independence?

- What does all of this mean for Britain and British national identity?

To start answering these questions we will need to go back further than 1979, and probe the origins and character of Scottish national identity more deeply.

5.1   A short history of Scotland

To begin answering the first set of questions – as to what happened to the Scottish nation and why it seemed so disinterested in ruling itself – we want to look at four moments in Scottish history: the feudal wars with England, the character of the Union, the invention of tartan, and the impact of industrialization.

5.1.1 Feudal wars

The idea of Scotland, its origins and meanings are, like Britishness, built around a few key pillars. In Scotland's case the medieval wars with England are one of these. The Scottish nation and national identity are to a great extent born of struggle against the English invader. The victories of William Wallace and Robert the Bruce, and the claims of independence and freedom are true enough. The *Declaration of Arbroath* (early fourteenth century), a key text of Scottish national identity, reads 'For as long as one hundred of us shall remain alive we shall never in any wise consent to submit to the rule of the English, for it is not for glory we fight, for riches, or for honours, but for freedom alone, which no good man loses but with his life'. But what kind of nation was being fought over? It is not at all clear whether the Scottish nation was present on the battlefields, or that the 'we' of the *Declaration of Arbroath* was the Scottish nation.

For most of the second half of the first millennium in what is now Scotland there existed a complex and shifting pattern of political power amongst minute feudal dynasties, Highland and island clans, and Scandinavian invaders. It was not until the eleventh century that something approaching a centralized Scottish state emerged with claims, if not the capacity, to police these dynasties and clans over most of the territory that is now Scotland. This Scottish state was little more than a small royal court, a minuscule bureaucracy, a few armed retainers and networks of patronage, and undefined borders. None the less, it was significant enough to attract repeated invasions from the south led by the English monarchy and the Norman aristocracy. The defeat of the English army of Edward II at Bannockburn (1314) sealed the survival of an independent Scottish aristocracy and ruling dynasty, but hardly a nation in the terms we outlined in Section 2. As for the *Declaration of Arbroath*, the 'we' refers to a small group of Scottish nobles who sent a letter to Pope John XXII. At the time the decisive issue was trying to persuade the Pope of the legitimacy of King Robert the Bruce who had been excommunicated at the behest of Edward I and to plead for Bruce's absolution and the effective recognition of his claim to rule.

5.1.2 Scotland and the Union

The Union of 1707 was a political and administrative union of parliaments, followed by a union of monarchies in 1714. If the Scottish nation had primarily consisted of court, dynasty, nobility and state prior to this, what, if anything, was left? In fact, a great deal. A distinct Scottish elite nation was preserved. The Union left the following untouched: an independent judicial system whose theory and practice was significantly different from English law; an independent Church of Scotland; an independent Scottish university and education system; and distinctive arrangements for local government. The sheer distance of London from Scotland in an era of unmechanized transport diminished England's cultural impact. For most of these elites a sense of

Scottishness was not incompatible with Britishness, particularly when buttressed by the economic and social gains to be made in the British Empire and British army. Indeed, the eighteenth century saw the emergence of the idea of North Britons amongst some of these elites.

5.1.3 The invention of tartan

The origins of tartan and the kilt are in the chequered cloth, cloaks and drapes of some Highland clans. Nations cannot be invented out of nothing and tartan has become emblematic of Scottish national distinctiveness. But formal Scottish national dress, and codified clan tartans, are all inventions, elaborations and codifications of the nineteenth century (Trevor-Roper, 1983). The process was initiated by Walter Scott who stage-managed the visit of George IV to Scotland (1822) and his audience with the remnants of the Highland clan elites in a riot of invented tartans. The British army, which drew heavily on the Highlands and indeed the whole of Scotland for recruits, created Scottish battle dress and military tartans, and sharp clothes manufacturers and salespeople invented genealogies and tartans for every occasion and surname. The embracing of tartan went hand-in-hand with a romantic evocation of the Highlands and its Gaelic culture as the heartland of an unconquered Scotland – Highland games, dancing, and landscape. Yet for most of the nineteenth century Highland culture and society was in a state of dislocation. Scottish and English landlords cleared the Highlands of much of its peasant crofter population. Gaelic was actively discouraged and Highland folk-culture deplored for its barbarity or naive simplicity.

5.1.4 Industrialization

What made a popular Scottish nation, and what paradoxically helped keep it part of the British nation-state, was the industrial revolution. At the time of the Union Scotland was an overwhelmingly agrarian society, by the late nineteenth century it was one of the most industrialized and advanced economies. Textiles and trade boomed on the back of access to imperial resources and markets; Glasgow grew rich on Virginian tobacco, Dundee on jute. Coal mining expanded and fed the fires of a large iron and steel industry. Engineering and shipbuilding followed, boosted by military and commercial shipping orders. For many upper- and middle-class Scots, as well as the skilled working class, the Union, Empire and Britain delivered prosperity and power. Calls for national independence and its mock tartan patriotism were bad for business and hopelessly antiquated. By the time the Scottish working class got the vote (mainly after 1918) their main political representative – the Labour Party – was predominantly unionist (though it has had its share of nationalists and radicals).

Even so, industrialization, mass education and popular publishing, and improved communications to the distant Highlands all led to a steady diffusion of Scottish narratives and symbols creating an awareness of similarities within Scotland and the differences between Scottish and English national identities. Simultaneously, industrialization created new divisions within Scottish society. Industrialization and urbanization were concentrated in the central belt of Scotland; most of the Borders, and the Highlands and islands remained agrarian economies. Working-class Glaswegians shared little of the world or the identities of the remaining Highland crofters or lowland farmers. Industrialization also brought a great wave of Catholic Irish immigration as cheap labour to the Scottish central belt. There they encountered fiercely Protestant employers and a Protestant urban working class. Religious and sectarian identities remain important features of the Scottish landscape.

ACTIVITY 4.6

What light, if any, do our three models of nations in Section 2 (Gellner, Anderson, Smith) shed on these four movements of Scottish history?

COMMENT

- Anderson's and Gellner's work indicate the importance of an elite national culture as the starting point for creating a mass national culture and identity.

- Smith's approach highlights the importance of Scotland's pre-modern ethnic cores, communities and territories, and the raw material it has generated for evoking and symbolizing Scottish national culture and identity.

- Gellner's account of homogenization and industrialization accounts for both the consolidation of a mass of popular Scottish national identity and the marginalization and disappearance of the Gaelic language and many aspects of Highland cultures.

- Anderson's idea that a nation is an 'imagined community' could be applied to Scotland by arguing that Scottish nationalism only managed to progressively turn into a mass movement once the country was industrialized, significant parts of the male population had been conscripted and its population became literate: only then could popular accounts of Scottish origins and history be diffused.

- However, none of these accounts acknowledge the ways in which Scottish industrialization undercut the formation of nations by creating class and sectarian divisions that were more significant for identities than the division between Scotland and England.

So in answer to our first question – what happened to the Scottish nation after the Union? – it was consolidated and enlarged. Building on a core of distinct civic institutions and elite identities, fundamentally defined by differentiation from England, a mass popular Scottish nation emerged. Cultural traditions were rescued, plundered and reinvented by romantic nationalist intellectuals. Industrialization delivered the death blow to peripheral cultures and identities.

Why was Scotland disinclined to rule itself? Three key reasons. First, because for most of the nineteenth and twentieth centuries the Union and Britishness delivered prosperity and status (see Section 3). Second, because uneven industrialization in Scotland created more significant internal fault lines of politics and identity between regions, classes, and cities than the external fault lines between Scotland and England. Third, because the retention of independent Scottish civic institutions and distance from Westminster meant that it did rule itself most of the time.

5.2 Scottish national identity and nationalism at the end of the twentieth century

So what reversed the situation? How can we explain the rise of Scottish nationalism and what role did the culture of a changing Scottish national identity play in this? Again, the answer to this question is complex and fiercely contested by Scots, social scientists and historians. At least four factors have helped shape this shift in identities and allegiances.

5.2.1 Economic change: oil and de-industrialization

While economics was never the only nor necessarily decisive factor in holding the Union together, it remained important. From the First World War onwards the structure and fortunes of the Scottish and English economies grew apart. Scotland's early heavy industries (coal, steel, shipbuilding) steadily contracted in size and global competitiveness. Few of the new industries, such as chemicals, cars and light engineering, established themselves in Scotland. Simultaneously, the benefits of Empire shrank with the Empire itself, and arguments for a distinctive Scottish economic policy became more appealing. The impact of the discovery of North Sea oil on Scottish politics and culture is built on this – nationalists made great play of the possibilities of Scottish financial independence and the inequities of billions of pounds of tax revenues flowing south.

5.2.2 Political marginalization

The case against independence had partly turned on the idea that politically Westminster, in fact, delivered a good deal to Scotland. The distribution of public expenditure across Britain was favourably tilted towards Scotland. Scotland was over-represented in terms of Westminster MPs per head of the population, and the Scottish Office provided a degree of autonomy. Seventeen years of Conservative government changed all of this. The reforms of the Thatcher era bit deeply into the popular fabric of Scottish politics and culture. The recession in the early 1980s was sharper, harder and longer in Scotland than in England. The boom that followed was slower and shallower. The contraction and privatization of the public sector met with much greater popular resistance. The dominant popular and political culture of Scotland was revealed as more collectivist and social democratic than Thatcher's individualistic and conservative middle England. This disparity became sharper with each election (see Table 4.1). The process was solidified and dramatized by the introduction of the Community Charge (poll tax) to Scotland before England and the extraordinary popular, but largely peaceful, resistance to the tax in Scotland. However, it was only when the English protested, and protested violently, that the Community Charge collapsed. Scottish MPs could never win the argument in a parliament dominated by English Conservatives. Other options were therefore considered.

TABLE 4.1   Number of Scottish MPs elected in British General Elections, 1983–97, by party

	Labour	Conservative	Liberal	SNP
1983	43	20	7	3
1987	50	10	9	3
1992	49	11	9	3
1997	56	0	10	6

5.2.3 The SNP and the reinvention of Scottish nationalism

The Scottish Nationalist Party was not established until 1928. For most of its first 30 years it was, at best, a peripheral force in Scottish politics and Scottish culture, confined to very narrow pockets of predominantly rural support, and, at worst, it was considered a political laughing stock, trading on an antiquated, invented imagery of Scotland that was long gone if it had ever existed at all. The combination of economic change and political marginalization described above opened a window of opportunity for the SNP. Revitalized by a younger generation of politicians, the SNP has successfully reinvented itself and its notion of Scottish nationalism to capitalize on this.

On the one hand the SNP has provided a home for disaffected voters from both sides by claiming a plague on both Conservative and Labour houses. On the other hand it has broadened its social and geographical appeal from its

Highland and north-east Scottish heartlands. It has moved cautiously to the left, seeking to capture both progressive middle-class urban votes and the labour-voting working class of the central belt, while holding on to its more conservative supporters. Simultaneously, the SNP tried to define and present Scottish national identity as progressive and modern, shunning excessive tartanry, and as **civic nationalism** (shared allegiance to institutions and culture) rather than **ethnic nationalism** (based on shared racial origins). But in the end the SNP is only one small contributor to Scottish culture and Scottish identity. While it has become the main opposition to Labour's dominance of Scottish politics, it is not at all clear that it has decisively tipped the balance of opinion from home rule to independence. Moreover, the SNP, like other political movements in Scotland, must also respond to a broader pattern of cultural change.

5.2.4 Cultural change and national identity

Here the messages are complex and sometimes confusing. Forces ranged against a successful civic nationalism include the sharp geographical and cultural differences between lowlands, the central belt and Highland Scotland; between Catholic and Protestant traditions; and between Glasgow and Edinburgh. Scotland has also acquired a significant black and Asian population for the first time. Anti-Englishness and racism are present. Against this there is another mood, that is confidence in civic nationalism and an open, plural and relaxed feeling towards cultural nationalism. Pat Kane (1999) describes the return home of one Scot, long emigrated to London: 'Expecting a nation tortuously writhing with the agonies of self-definition and cultural identity, he found a "who cares" mentality. Tartan can be worn without hand wringing ... bangra wedding bands from London can easily follow Viking longboats down hogmanay processions in Edinburgh'. Whether in the longer term the creation of a Scottish parliament can create a framework and a politics that appeals to these kinds of Scots and Scottishness, and if not whether only an independent nation-state can do so, remains to be seen.

Civic nationalism
A nationalist project in which citizenship and membership of the nation is based on residence and allegiance to the ruling civic and political institutions and not on race, ethnicity or language.

Ethnic nationalism
A nationalist project in which citizenship and membership of the nation is determined by ethnic origin alone, irrespective of political and cultural allegiances and length of residence in a nation.

SUMMARY

- Since the Union there has been support for the Union, for devolution and for independence within Scotland.

- The balance of power and opinion lay with the Union for most of the last 300 years, as the Union was successful and British national identity was attractive.

- A combination of declining economic fortunes and distinct Scottish political cultures has helped open the way for both a new form of Scottish national identity and a Scottish nationalist politics.

6 UNCERTAIN NATION, DIVERSE NATION: WHAT IS ENGLAND?

The last of the three questions we posed about the transformation of Scottish national identity was: what does this mean for Britain? Of course, the impact of change in Scotland cannot be separated from changes in Northern Ireland, Wales and Europe. In all of these cases the centrality and certainties of Britishness have been challenged, alternative identities have become stronger and drained Britishness of some of its earlier power and coherence. If Britain is losing its Celtic periphery what remains? What remains is what has always been the dominant component of Britain and Britishness: England and Englishness.

ACTIVITY 4.7

Look at Figures 4.8 and 4.9. Which, if any, best characterizes England and Englishness today?

FIGURE 4.8
Cricket on the green

FIGURE 4.9
Football fans

COMMENT _____

Figure 4.8 looks like one very particular, albeit very widespread, set of English images: rural, male, undisturbed, peaceful, white and upper class.

The photo of the fans seems more appropriate today: urban, popular, rough and ready rather than manicured, comic rather than pompous – who else but the English would embellish their flag with a phrase which includes the words 'eating ... pie'? However, it is a limited and narrow version of Englishness, for us at any rate. It is exclusively white and exclusively male.

_____

Uncertainties about Britishness are forcing the English to rediscover and redefine themselves. How is it that some of the dominant cultural representations and accounts of Englishness seem antiquated or irrelevant? Why is it that the England football team has acquired such a central place in the construction and celebration of English national identity? These are, of course, enormously complex questions. We touch on three issues here.

6.1 Alternative Englands?

As we already know the dominant social and cultural component of the early British nation was the English aristocracy. Many of the most potent symbols and representations of Englishness continue to reflect this. It is not only cricket and village greens. Englishness is stately homes, rolling countryside (with no right of access), pomp and ceremony, afternoon tea, Ascot, and Wimbledon, etc. Of course, all of these things continue to exist and are part of the fabric of Englishness, but they come from and speak to an age and a social order that has almost completely disappeared. The English aristocracy's grip on economic, political and cultural power was already faltering in the decades before the First World War. The economic and personal costs of the war, the rise of the labour movement, and the precipitous decline in agriculture in the inter-war years finished the English aristocracy off as the dominant player in English social and political life (Cannadine, 1990). The monarchy, at the apex of this class and culture, survived by reinventing itself again: from imperial monarchs to head of the commonwealth, and from distant rulers to a public pageant of family values. But the relentless scrutiny of the popular press and culture has cruelly exposed the frailty of this analogy.

However, the historical and cultural cupboard is not entirely empty for the English. There are, and have been for some time, diverse alternative historical and cultural accounts of England being told or waiting to be told, for example, there is a popular, radical and liberal English tradition. In the wake of the Civil War (1642–49) England effectively invented the modern liberal programme of limited, accountable constitutional government. English intellectuals were at the forefront of modern conceptions of liberty, the rule of law and representative democracy. English radicals, like Tom Paine and John Wilkes, argued for these notions to be turned into enduring political structures in the eighteenth and nineteenth centuries, as did suffragettes in the twentieth century. Although universal suffrage was not achieved until 1929, England has never fostered or fallen to an authoritarian dictatorship.

There is also, in contrast to the insularity of some notions of Englishness, a cosmopolitan England. An England that for centuries welcomed foreigners, harboured asylum seekers and refugees, that travelled widely and drew generally on other cultures. This is an England of import and export, of goods, people and ideas – Blackpool Tower is a clone of the Eiffel Tower, the new German Reichstag in Berlin was designed by an Englishman.

6.2 Multi-cultural England?

England in both the photographs in Activity 4.7 is white. But England on the football pitch and in the demographic statistics is an ethnically mixed, multi-cultural society. The 1991 census, which was the first to include a question on ethnicity, indicated that 5.5 per cent (just over 3 million people) of the UK population identified themselves as belonging to one of the ethnic groups which did not include white people. The 2001 census is likely to show an increase on this.

TABLE 4.2 Ethnic composition of the population of Great Britain, 1991 (thousands of persons)

OPCS[a] ethnic group	Great Britain	England	Wales	Scotland
White	51,843.9	44,114.6	2,793.3	4,936.1
Black – Caribbean	499.1	496.3	2.7	0.0
Black – African	207.5	203.2	2.3	2.0
Black – Other	178.5	172.9	3.5	2.4
Indian	840.8	823.9	6.7	10.2
Pakistani	475.8	448.8	5.8	21.2
Bangladeshi	160.3	156.1	3.4	0.8
Chinese	157.5	142.4	4.9	10.2
Other – Asian	196.7	189.7	3.5	3.5
Other – Other	290.1	273.3	7.7	9.2
All minorities	3,006.5	2,906.5	40.5	59.5
Total population	54,860.2	47,026.5	2,835.1	4,998.6

[a] Office of Population and Census Studies.
Source: Owen, 1993

Immigration to Britain is not entirely new. French Huguenot Protestants settled in Britain during the reformation. Africans, many arriving as house slaves, have lived in Britain since the eighteenth century. In the nineteenth and early twentieth centuries Eastern Europeans, Jews and Italians settled in England, and as we know from Scotland, large numbers of Irish immigrants crossed the Irish Sea. But the scale and the consequences of the post-Second World War migrations have been different. First, they have been significantly larger. Second, unlike the invisible white migrations of the previous 150 years, these were very visible black migrations from the ex-imperial colonies of the new commonwealth. 'Black', in this sense, is a highly contested term. As you can see from Table 4.2, these migrant communities display an enormous internal diversity: ethnic Hindu Indians displaced from East Africa, Muslims from Bangladesh and Pakistan, and Christian African-Caribbeans from a multitude of different islands. Different migrant communities have tended to concentrate in particular cities and distinct areas of cities though, as you can see from Table 4.2, they are overwhelmingly concentrated in England. There are considerable differences in the economic experience of different groups and significant stratification within groups. 'Black' has been used by and applied to these groups to signal a collective difference from the white European majority and a collective experience of difference that has been consistently marked by exclusion and racism.

What does this mean for notions of national identity? Broadly speaking most of these migrant communities have acquired full British citizenship. Attempting to reverse this kind of formal civic nationalism and replace it with an exclusivist white ethnic British nationalism has been the goal of the fascist far right in the UK. Violence and intimidation notwithstanding, it has made little political headway. Will the decline of Britishness and the uncertainties of Englishness provide a new opportunity for the emergence of an English ethnic nationalism? Or can an English civic nationalism accommodate itself to the kind of cultural pluralism that these migrations have created? Can Englishness be a **multi-cultural** diverse national identity?

There are many reasons why this might be problematic, but two of the central issues are racism and historical narratives. They are connected. As we know from Chapters 2 and 3, life chances, income, power, educational experience and opportunity all display systematic patterns of inequality between the genders and social classes. A similar conclusion can be arrived at for different ethnic groups (Modood *et al.*, 1997). Some minority ethnic groups (Jews and Indians, for example) appear more successful than the white Christian majority ethnic group. However, for most groups the experience is the reverse. As we also know from Chapters 2 and 3, *stereotyping* and *labelling* are key cultural processes by which majority and dominant groups can define, demean and disempower minorities and subordinate groups. But it is not just in day-to-day, private and personal encounters that this kind of racism manifests itself (see Jackie Kay's poem in Chapter 1, Section 7). In 1999, the Macpherson report on the murder of Stephen Lawrence (the black teenager stabbed in a racist assault in south London) found there was

Multi-cultural
A society in which civic nationalism and multi-ethnic citizenship is accompanied by public recognition and equal esteem for a diversity of ethnic groups and cultures.

Institutionalized racism
Systematic, structural and patterned forms of discrimination, intentional and unintentional on the basis of race/ethnicity, generated by the organization, culture, predispositions and actions of an institution.

overwhelming evidence not only of police incompetence in their handling of the murder inquiry, but of **institutionalized racism** in the Metropolitan police force (The Stationery Office, 1999). The resonance of the report has touched every institution in the country.

How does this connect with historical narratives? Stereotypes, labels and prejudice, like nations, cannot be invented out of nothing. Of course, the roots of racism are complex and multi-faceted, but part of their explanation lies in the historical encounter and story of Britain with non-European societies; a story, as we know from Section 3, that was imperial. The subjugation and colonization of non-European societies has been legitimized and explained in terms of the opposition between an advanced civilized Christian white Britain/England and a backward barbarian pagan black colonial peoples. It is hard to counter racism, let alone evoke a successful multi-culturalism, while these narratives and explanations are at the core of Britishness and Englishness. Perhaps England has a choice: to cling to or try and ignore these imperial narratives or to rewrite the colonial experience in different less **ethnocentric** terms incorporating and acknowledging, alongside stories of exploration, discovery and world power, the parallel narratives of slavery and dispossession.

Ethnocentric
A belief or view or understanding that privileges the culture and perspective of one ethnic group to the detriment or exclusion of others.

6.3 Civic nationalism without civic institutions

If Englishness can no longer rely on simplistic and racist notions of ethnic nationalism, nor continue to meaningfully draw on the stock of aristocratic and rural culture to define itself, then could these alternative Englands, like Scotland, build upon national distinctive civil institutions to fashion a new, multi-cultural, diverse, national identity?

Can you think of any distinctively and exclusively English national institutions?

It is actually quite hard to do so. We came up with English National Opera (which performs opera in English) and English Heritage (which manages old buildings). Hardly the stuff of a coherent popular national identity or the base for constructing a civic nationalism. The political and legal systems that govern England include Wales, as does the university system. The Church of England is independent and English, but in a predominantly secular and a multi-faith society, it is not a very promising foundation.

Some have responded to this dilemma by calling for the creation of new and distinctive English political institutions – an English parliament for example. However, it seems that if a new sense of Englishness is tentatively emerging, it is emerging in the realm of popular culture. It is a popular culture that exhibits some elements of a cosmopolitan England. England today, particularly for the post-1960s generations, is an urban society, ethnically and regionally diverse with very distinctive forms and mixes of popular music, poetry and literature, and television and film culture. England is a whole host of things, *Coronation Street* and *EastEnders*, The Beatles and Oasis, Benjamin Zephaniah and Martin Amis, home improvements and garden makeovers. England might reinvent itself on a diet of high art, suburban DIY and urban popular culture as a diverse nation. Whether it could be true to a liberal, radical, democratic England remains to be seen. The potential for a revival of racist and ethnic forms of nationalism remains alive. Richard Weight is optimistic that the English might achieve this peaceful diversity, but that in the absence of formal civic institutions the English will have to rely on the England football team to bind them together.

FIGURE 4.10 The future of English civic nationalism?: Paul Ince and Alan Shearer at the 1998 World Cup

On my way to watch England play Argentina something happened that was ... significant. I was walking down a busy road in South London carrying a large George flag. The Stephen Lawrence Inquiry was being held not far away at the Elephant and Castle, and black newspapers were full of letters lamenting the virulent racism that still exists in England. Yet, when a dozen West Indian mothers outside a school saw my flag, they smiled and waved and their children broke into a chant of 'Eng-er-land'; an Asian man in a car honked his horn and gave me a thumbs up ... I doubt that the Union Jack would have got the same response even if a British team had existed because, for most blacks and Asians, it retains echoes of empire and the National Front. The Cross of St. George is more neutral, inclusive symbol ... and more clearly offers a right to belong to this country.

(Weight, 1999)

We shall see.

REFERENCES

Anderson, B. (1983) *Imagined Communities: Reflections on the Origins and Spread of Nationalism*, London, Verso.

Barthes, R. (1972) *Mythologies*, London, Cape.

Boal, F.W. (1995) *Shaping a City: Belfast in the Late Twentieth Century*, Belfast, The Institute of Irish Studies, The Queen's University of Belfast.

Cannadine, D. (1990) *The Decline and Fall of the British Aristocracy*, New Haven, Yale University Press.

Colley, L. (1992) *Britons: Forging the Nation, 1707–1837*, New Haven, Yale University Press.

Durkheim, E. (1915) *The Elementary Forms of the Religious Life: A Study in Religious Sociology* (translated by Swain, J.), London, Allen and Unwin.

Gellner, E. (1983) *Nations and Nationalism*, Oxford, Blackwell.

Guibernau, M. (1998) *Nationalisms*, Cambridge, Polity.

Harvie, C. (1998) *Scotland and Nationalism: Scottish Society and Politics, 1707 to the Present*, London, Routledge.

Kane, P. (1999) 'From Brave Heart to cosmo-Scotia', *New Statesman*, 19 March.

Lynch, M. (1992) *Scotland: A New History*, London, Pimlico.

Marr, A. (1992) *The Battle for Scotland*, Harmondsworth, Penguin.

Modood, T. *et al.* (1997) *Ethnic Minorities in Britain: Diversity and Disadvantage*, London, Policy Studies Institute.

Owen, D. (1993) 'Local census data for ethnic groups in Great Britain', *New Community*, vol.19, no.2.

Parker, T. (1994) *May the Lord in His Mercy be Kind to Belfast*, London, HarperCollins.

Rose, G. (1990) 'Place and identity: a sense of place' in Massey, D. and Jess, P. (eds) *A Place in the World?*, Oxford, Oxford University Press.

Smith, A.D. (1986) *The Ethnic Origin of Nations*, Oxford, Blackwell.

Smith, A.D. (1995) *Nations and Nationalism in a Global Era*, Cambridge, Polity.

The Stationery Office (1999) *Sir William Macpherson's Inquiry into Matters Arising From the Death of Stephen Lawrence on 22nd April 1993*, London, The Stationery Office.

Trevor-Roper, H. (1983) 'The invention of tradition: the Highland tradition of Scotland' in Hobsbawm, E. and Ranger, T. (eds) *The Invention of Tradition*, Cambridge, Cambridge University Press.

Weight, R. (1999) 'Raise St. George's standard high', *New Statesman*, 8 January.

FURHER READING

The literature of nations and nationalism is very large, as is the literature on Britain, Britishness and other national identities in the British Isles. Some of the most accessible texts have been referenced in this chapter. On theories and definitions of nationalism and national identity Benedict Anderson's *Imagined Communities* is short and readable, but focused on the experience of South-East Asia. Eric Hobsbawm's *Nations and Nationalism since 1780* has a more European focus.

On the making of Britishness, Linda Colley's *Britons* is unsurpassed, although it is being steadily corrected by a great wave of historical work that it has helped inspire. On contemporary British identities a good place to start is Susan Bassenet (ed.) *Studying British Culture*. Irish national identities, introduced in Tony Parker's work, can be placed in a more rigorous historical framework by looking at Roy Foster's *Modern Ireland*, while the origins and interaction of multiple sources of identity in Northern Ireland are explored in Joseph Ruane and Jennifer Todd's *The Dynamics of Conflict in Northern Ireland*. Wales and Welsh national identity, which has had a rather raw deal in this chapter, can be explored in R. Jenkins' *Rethinking Ethnicity*. On ethnicity and race in the UK, the facts, figures and key issues are all covered in Tariq Modood and Richard Berthouds' *Ethnic Minorities in Britain: Diversity and Disadvantage*, the fourth national survey of minority ethnic groups.

Bassenet, S. (ed.) (1997) *Studying British Culture: An Introduction*, London, Routledge.

Foster, R. (1988) *Modern Ireland, 1600–1972*, Harmondsworth, Penguin.

Hobsbawm, E. (1992) *Nations and Nationalism since 1780: Programme, Myth, Reality*, Cambridge, Cambridge University Press.

Jenkins, R. (ed.) (1997) *Rethinking Ethnicity*, London, Sage.

Ruane, J. and Todd, J. (1996) *The Dynamics of Conflict in Northern Ireland: Power, Conflict and Emancipation*, Cambridge, Cambridge University Press.

Afterword

Kath Woodward

This book has, as it promised, been question led. In the 'Introduction' I posed three framing questions. The discussion has addressed these questions by focusing on the contributions of different social scientists, whose responses have in themselves generated more questions. How do we make sense of ourselves as individuals in relation to the social world which we inhabit? When the world changes do we remain constant or does who we are change too and how does this happen?

Now I want to return to my framing questions, starting with the first one: *how are identities formed?*

The processes involved in taking up identities require some connections between individuals and the world in which they live. We have to be recruited into an identity, which involves some kind of active engagement on our part. Do you remember the football example in Chapter 1? More importantly, as was argued in Chapter 4, there are points in time when people identify with the nation and actively take up a national identity. How are we recruited into these identities? One important aspect of the process is the way in which people represent themselves and recognize others. We use symbols, such as language, clothes, flags, badges, to mark ourselves as having the same identity as one group of people and a different identity from the others.

Identity is always in some way marked by difference and sameness. Identity relies upon individuals' understanding of these symbolic markers, whether of gender categories, or class identity, or national or ethnic identities. Differences may be stereotyped and involve an exaggerated selection of defining characteristics or, as we saw with the fuzzy categories in Chapter 2, they may be much more complex and subtle, as well as involving contradiction and conflict. In order to identify with an identity position we have to be able to imagine ourselves as occupying that position; that is, to think of ourselves, in our heads, as British or Irish, as the good mother, the successful career person, as streetwise, as female or as male. As we saw in Chapter 2, the process of forming a gender identity is not only influenced by our biology. Children have to understand the categories through which their own society classifies femininity and masculinity and to pick up the appropriate clues.

Sometimes the process of recruitment might even be unconscious. We may not be fully aware of why we appear to have embraced a particular identity. The process of identification is complex and can involve the operation of factors which are part of our own personal histories, such as early childhood experience. At times there may be a moment of recognition in the identification process, where we may not be quite sure why we think 'that's me', but it just seems right. The concept of interpellation offers some insight into what is going on when people recognize themselves; for example, in advertisements or in political recruiting material.

Many of the approaches which have been explored in this book have emphasized the social aspects of the identity equation. Although as individuals we have to identify – that is, to take up an identity actively – there are also structures in the social world with which we identify. Some structures, picked out in Chapter 1, were explored in more detail in the following chapters. Gender is an important aspect of identity. Even very young children need to know whether they are a girl or a boy. Gender categories are constructed through our biological bodies and through social and cultural classificatory systems. At some points in history, class identity has been very important. These identities involve individuals recognizing their own class position and having some degree of class consciousness, which is also acknowledged by others. Traditional views of identity, including the Marxist and Weberian approaches to class, have emphasized the role of social structures in shaping people's identities. More recent approaches have stressed the interaction between the social and the personal, such as when individuals and groups negotiate their identities and represent themselves through patterns of consumption. Ethnicity and race are also social structures which influence the identities which people can adopt. However, these structures are changing and may be renegotiated. Identities are not fixed; they are fluid and both individuals and social structures are changing.

How much scope is there for the negotiation of identities? Are we limited to a great extent by our bodies, by our economic circumstances, by the social construction and stereotypes of gender and ethnicity? Can people exercise some agency in the creation of their collective and individual identities?

This leads in to our next framing question about the relationship between agency and structure: *to what extent can we shape our own identities?*

I have argued that there has to be some active engagement on our part in taking up identities. However, as has been shown throughout the book, there are severe constraints on the degree of agency which we may be able to exercise. For example, economic circumstances, changes in employment, poverty, racism and lack of recognition of our ethnic or national identities all deny us access to identities which we might want to take up. Cultural construction of gender, social regulation and even legal categories prevent individuals from taking up alternative identities. Social attitudes towards ethnic diversity can limit its celebration by those who are constructed as outsiders. Our own bodies put limits on what it is possible to achieve. However the interrelationship between the personal and the social involves negotiation. People reconstruct their own identities, even within the constraints of poverty. Through the collective action of social movements, of class-based action, and through asserting ethnic identities and separate national identities within a multicultural UK, people reshape the social structures which restrict them. Even at the level of the individual, through body projects, it is possible to recreate our identities through transforming our bodies, by getting fit, by challenging stereotypes.

This leads to our third framing question: *are there more uncertainties about identity at this moment in the UK?*

The book has presented several examples of social change in the contemporary UK. Certainties about employment, especially male employment in manufacturing industry, about family life and gender roles, and the ethnic and national composition of the UK itself have shifted in the period since the Second World War. There has been a move away from class-based identities and the security that might have been afforded by particular patterns of employment and the associated gendered roles within families. In one sense these changes can be seen as indicating greater uncertainty. Contemporary concerns with identity can be seen as focusing on presenting ourselves to others, through consuming identities, and through lifestyle and developing ourselves as individuals. This can be contrasted with the changing ways in which collective identities have been forged – for example, through class identification. New social movements have produced a new focus for the politics of collective identities, with their concerns with gender, sexuality and race, in some instances making 'the personal political'. Uncertainties can also be expressed as responses to change and the opportunities for diversity which are offered. In the twenty-first century there is a greater diversity of forms of domestic living than in the 1950s. Gender stereotypes are challenged by reconstructions and more fluid identities. The UK is a multicultural society, albeit one which still manifests the constraints of racism. There is legislative as well as cultural recognition of the separate identities of Irish, Scottish and Welsh peoples within the UK. Uncertainty and diversity coexist.

This book has also been about social science knowledge and its production. We began with questions which we have revisited and to which we have added several more. This illustrates areas of the process of social science enquiry. We started with questions but quickly moved on to claims: claims about identity and how it was defined. In order to find out we looked at a variety of evidence. The book has offered a range of evidence, both quantitative and qualitative. One source of evidence which was cited in Chapter 1 involved a personal narrative, the testimony of an individual. This raised other questions about the need for additional evidence as well as the need to ask more questions about one person's account. What else could social science tell us? What were the social elements involved. We suggested class and gender at this point, and these are structures which Chapters 2 and 3 explored in more detail. Chapter 2 unpacked some of the meanings of gender and offered evidence of how ideas about gender identities are produced. Chapter 3 presented empirical evidence about the distribution of wealth, with some powerful representations of data; for example, in the income parade. In order to evaluate the evidence, we looked at different theoretical approaches within the social sciences. The inclusion of some factors – gender in Chapter 2 and class and economic factors in Chapter 3 –

also highlights the exclusion of others. One of the important questions posed in evaluating the evidence involves asking what is missing. Where we come from, in particular, ethnicity and place, are key elements on making sense of who we are. Chapter 4's discussion of ethnicity and the ways in which meanings are produced about identity by placing it, in terms of time, history and place, adds another component to the circuit of our social science investigation of identity. This chapter also makes more explicit the concerns with culture introduced in Chapter 1.

Throughout the book we have indicated some of the ways in which representation is a key component in linking the personal to the social. Meanings about gender, class and ethnicity are produced through their representation within culture. Children learn how to categorize through gendered representations of dress and behaviour. These symbolic systems are what we use in everyday interactions. This is how we categorize other people as being the same as us or as different from us. As we saw in Chapter 3, meanings about poverty and about what constitutes poverty are represented through culture, although those who experience it may challenge these representations, especially of being victims, and struggle to redefine themselves within these cultural constraints. In the histories of the nation, for example of the English and the Scottish, in Chapter 4, we saw more explicitly how ideas about national identity are created through symbols, such as the flag, through rituals, ranging from affairs of state and the activities of the monarch to sporting events, as well as through the ways in which the nation constructs its past and names its heroes.

We started with questions and have added several more to the initial framing three. We have suggested ways in which social scientists address these questions. We have offered some claims about identity and some ways of supporting and evaluating these claims. The book has addressed some of the important aspects of identity and indicated some of the complex ways in which identities are formed, stressing the importance of the interaction between the personal and the social. There are no simple answers. There are tensions between the personal and the social and between the agency people can exert and the constraints of social structures. There are uncertainties, which are historically specific. We live in changing times. We have multiple identities and identities are multifaceted. Multiple identities offer the possibility of diversity and have the potential for reconstruction and renewal. This is why identity matters.

Acknowledgements

Grateful acknowledgement is made to the following sources for permission to reproduce material in this book.

Chapter 1

Text

Kay, J. (1991) 'So you think I'm a mule?', *The Adoption Papers*, Sheba Feminist Publishers. Copyright © 1991 Jackie Kay.

Figures

Figure 1.1: examples of UK passports. Crown copyright is reproduced with the permission of the Controller of Her Majesty's Stationery Office; Figure 1.2: ICI Alkathene advert from *Ideal Home* magazine, August 1956. © The Advertising Archives; Figure 1.3: from 'Working on it', editorial in *Pregnancy and Birth*, July 1998. Courtesy of *Mother and Baby* Picture Library. Photo: Telegraph Colour Library; Figures 1.4 and 1.6: Martin Jenkinson/Report Digital; Figure 1.5(top): Football League Division 1, Official Programme, 7 October 1961. Front cover by kind permission of W.E.A., South Yorkshire District; Figure 1.5(bottom): National Coal Board advertisement by kind permission of W.E.A., South Yorkshire District; Figure 1.7: Nick Cobbing/Report Digital; Figure 1.8: Brenda Prince/Format; Figure 1.9: Maggie Murray/Format; Figure 1.10: Andi Faryl Schreiber/Format; Figure 1.11: Chris Barry; Figure 1.12: Copyright © Age Concern England.

Illustration

p.16: 'True self' by Chris Madden. Copyright © Paperlink Ltd, London 1999.

Chapter 2

Text

Curtis, R., Elton, B., Lloyd, J. and Atkinson, R. (1998) *Blackadder: The Whole Damn Dynasty*, pp.123/124, Michael Joseph. *Blackadder II* copyright © Richard Curtis and Ben Elton, 1985. This collection copyright © Richard Curtis, Ben Elton, John Lloyd and Rowan Atkinson, 1998. Reproduced by permission of Penguin Books Ltd, London.

Figures

Figure 2.1: Birth Certificate. © Crown Copyright. Published by permission of the Controller of Her Majesty's Stationery Office and the Office for National Statistics; Figure 2.2: Turner, P.J. (1995) *Sex, Gender and Identity*, The British Psychological Society; Figure 2.3: © Mike Levers/The Open University; Figure 2.5: Bright, M. (1998) 'Boys performing badly', *The Observer*, 4 January 1998. Copyright © *The Observer*; Figure 2.6: Kimura, D. (1992) 'Sex differences in the brain', *Scientific American*, September 1992. Courtesy of Jared Schneidman Design; Figure 2.8:

© Hector Breeze. From *The Guardian*, 7 January 1998; Figure 2.9: Sally and Richard Greenhill; Figure 2.10: Garry Fry/Barnaby's Picture Library; Figures 2.11 and 2.12: Murphy, P. and Elwood, J. (1998) 'Gendered experiences, choices and achievement – exploring the links', *International Journal of Inclusive Education*, vol.2, no.2, Taylor and Francis Ltd, PO Box 25, Abingdon, Oxfordshire OX14 3UE.

Cartoon

p.49: © LEEDSpostcards.

Chapter 3

Figures

Figure 3.1: © Ian Jackson, *The Guardian*, 15 January 1999; Figure 3.2: Stephen Mansfield/*The Scotsman*; Figures 3.3, 3.7 and 3.10: John Harris/Report Digital; Figure 3.5: Goodman, A. and Webb, S. (1994) *For Richer, For Poorer: The Changing Distribution of Income in the United Kingdom, 1961–91, Commentary No.42*, Institute for Fiscal Studies; Figure 3.6: Department of Social Security (1997) *Households Below Average Income, A Statistical Analysis 1979–1994/5*. Crown Copyright is reproduced with the permission of the Controller of Her Majesty's Stationery Office; Figure 3.8: *The Guardian*, 15 January 1999/British Election Study; Figure 3.9: Jess Hurd/*Socialist Worker*; Figure 3.11: Don McPhee/*The Guardian*, 9 November 1998.

Cartoon

p.105: © Steve Bell/*The Guardian*, 15 January 1999.

Chapter 4

Text

Parker, T. (1993) *May the Lord in His Mercy be Kind to Belfast*, Jonathan Cape. Copyright © Tony Parker 1993.

Figures

Figure 4.1: Boal, F.W. (1995) *Shaping a City: Belfast in the Late Twentieth Century*, The Institute of Irish Studies, The Queen's University of Belfast/The Northern Ireland Housing Executive. © F.W. Boal and The Northern Ireland Housing Executive; Figure 4.5: © Andrew Testa/*The Guardian*, 6 September 1997; Figure 4.6: Ian Waldie/Popperfoto; Figures 4.7 and 4.8: Popperfoto; Figures 4.9 and 4.10: Bob Thomas/Popperfoto.

Table

Table 4.2: Owen, D. (1993) 'Local census data for ethnic groups in Great Britain', *New Community*, vol.19, no.2, Taylor and Francis Ltd, PO Box 25, Abingdon, Oxfordshire OX14 3UE.

Cover

Image copyright © 1996 PhotoDisc, Inc.

Index